'An indispensable history, guide and primer on local elections in Ireland. The scholarship of the book is enhanced by its accessibility and readability. Highly recommended. Aodh Quinlivan and Liam Weeks are to be commended for this valuable addition to the canon.'
Harry McGee, Political Correspondent, *The Irish Times*

'In a country fascinated with the local dimension to national politics but without a properly functioning local government system this work illuminates the maze through which aspiring and serving councillors have to negotiate. It is a truly enjoyable and informative read for the new candidate and the experienced councillor. Above all it highlights what could be achieved if ever we have a reformed, energised and powerful local government system in Ireland.'
Dermot Lacey, Dublin city councillor and former Lord Mayor of Dublin

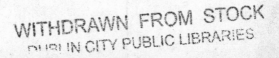

'This is a very interesting read, with some new insights into the electoral process, candidates, motivations etc. which I'm sure will make for great reading for candidates, journalists and pundits at the local elections.'
Dr Mark Callanan, Institute of Public Administration, Dublin

'This is a wonderful contribution to the local political scene in that it looks at issues which, up until this point, we have only been able to discuss on the basis of anecdotal evidence but now will have the researched answers to these matters. *All Politics is Local* is an entertaining and insightful read for all interested in local politics.'
Tom Ryan, Director of the Association of Municipal Authorities of Ireland

ALL POLITICS IS LOCAL

Liam Weeks lectures in politics in the Department of Government, University College Cork. A former Government of Ireland scholar, he has a PhD in political science from Trinity College Dublin. He has written on a variety of issues related to Irish politics and is co-editing a book on *Minor Parties in Irish Political Life*.

Aodh Quinlivan lectures in politics in the Department of Government, University College Cork. Prior to his appointment in UCC, Aodh worked in Cork County Council, and local government remains his primary area of research interest. Aodh has published widely in this field, including *Philip Monahan – A Man Apart* (Dublin, 2006) and *Innovation and Best Practice in Irish Local Government* (with Emmanuelle Schön-Quinlivan, Dublin, 2009).

ALL POLITICS IS LOCAL

A GUIDE TO LOCAL ELECTIONS IN IRELAND

Liam Weeks & Aodh Quinlivan

The Collins Press

FIRST PUBLISHED IN 2009 BY
The Collins Press
West Link Park
Doughcloyne
Wilton
Cork

British Library Cataloguing in Publication Data

Weeks, Liam.
All politics is local : a guide to local elections in
Ireland.
1. Local elections—Ireland. 2. Local government—
Ireland.
3. Ireland—Politics and government—21st century.
I. Title II. Quinlivan, Aodh.
324.9'4170824-dc22

ISBN-13: 9781848890022

Typesetting by Carrigboy Typesetting Services
Typeset in Berkeley Book
Printed in Great Britain by J F Print Ltd, Sparkford, Somerset

Contents

List of Tables and Figures

Acknowledgements

We are pleased to acknowledge the generous help of a variety of people who contributed positively to this book. We are especially grateful to those who gave us feedback and comments on different drafts and who offered us sound advice along the way. On this list are Professor Neil Collins, Tom O'Connor, Dick Haslam, Tim McCarthy, Dermot Lacey, Mark Callanan and Tom Ryan. We want to thank our colleagues in the Department of Government in University College Cork for their advice, support, encouragement and humour. Two visiting American students, Will Whitmore and Travis Johnson, were of enormous help in preparing this manuscript and their assistance is most appreciated. We express special thanks to Frank Daly and Eoin Corrigan in the Department of the Environment, Heritage and Local Government, to Michael Higgins in the Cork City and County Archives. We are hugely indebted to the staff at The Collins Press.

Liam: Extended thanks are due to all the local election candidates who completed a survey in July 2004, on which the data in chapters 5 and 6 is based. They put up with persistent phone calls, letters and postcards and without their support, neither this book nor my doctoral thesis would have been completed. Research on candidates and campaigns began for me with my PhD in Trinity College Dublin, and thanks are due to Professors Michael Gallagher and Michael Marsh in the Department of Political Science for their formal supervision and support during the process. I would also like to acknowledge the financial support of the Irish Research Council for the Humanities and Social Sciences for its awarding of a Government of Ireland postgraduate scholarship to complete my studies. I would like to thank Mícheál Ó Fathartaigh and Clive Ahern for their insights on local elections, both past and present. Finally, I want to thank Ania and my family, Graham, Margaret and Caoimhe, for their support in my career and life beyond the academic desk. This book is dedicated to them.

Aodh: I'm grateful to Liam for coming up with the idea for this book and including me on the project. I think we worked well together and I hope we can collaborate again in the future. I dedicate the book to the two people who give meaning to my life: my beautiful wife, Emmanuelle, and my wonderful son, Adam.

Liam Weeks & Aodh Quinlivan
April 2009

Preface

If elections are at the heart of politics, then voting is the first duty of democracy. Within any democratic system, local government plays a vital part in the pattern of government. The main virtue of government at this level is the fact that it is *local* and accessible to the general public. The easiest measurement of participation in local government is turnout at local elections and – as we will see in this book – turnout has fluctuated a lot in recent times. Despite a downward trend over the period from 1985 to 1999, the Irish local elections of 2004 drew 1.8 million people to the polls. This was the largest ever poll for local elections in Ireland. Irish local elections fulfil the functions classically associated with any elections, that is to recruit politicians, make (local) governments, provide representation, influence policy, educate voters and build legitimacy. But are local elections different from national elections? What influences people to stand for election for a county council seat? What type of person seeks local election and what campaign strategies do they typically employ? These are just some of the questions that we answer in this book and, in so doing, we hope to shine some light on a level of Irish democracy that is frequently ignored.

The title of the book is inspired by the favourite phrase of Thomas P. 'Tip' O'Neill, the Irish-American politician who served in the US House of Representatives for thirty-four years and who was Speaker of the House from 1977 to 1987. O'Neill's rise to the third most important political position in America, after the President and Vice-President, was built on a career of successful election campaigns over a fifty-year period. His basic belief was that to understand how a politician behaves, you must look at what issues affect her/him in her/his own constituency. The 'all politics is local' rule applies the world over but it is especially relevant in Ireland where we have a localised and highly personalised political culture.

This is the first book to look at Irish local government through the lens of local elections and it contains information that will be of use to the general public, existing and potential councillors and local government officials, as well as academics and students.

The first chapter sets the scene by making a case for local government and discussing the importance of local elections. Chapter 2 explains the history and structure of Irish local government. Knowledge of how the local government system operates is essential for both councillors and citizens. The rules governing local elections are presented in chapter 3. Among the questions answered are, who is entitled to stand for local election? Who is allowed to vote? How does the voting system work? Are there limits on campaign spending?

Chapter 4 describes local elections that have taken place at county and city level, from the first contests in 1899 to the twenty-second set of elections in 2004. The focus in chapter 5 is on the candidates who stand for local election. Do they exhibit the same characteristics as general election candidates or does a different kind of person come forward at local government level?

Chapter 6 examines the various approaches to campaigns adopted by local election candidates. For example, is it important to distribute posters and leaflets? How much money does the average local election candidate spend on her or his campaign? In chapter 7 we concentrate on local election results and investigate how political parties and Independents fare and assess how the results differ, if at all, from those at national general elections.

Our guide to local elections concludes with an epilogue in which we draw together conclusions from the previous seven chapters and analyse what political parties can learn from local elections. The central theme throughout the book is the significance of localism in the Irish political system. Politicians who ignore grass-roots developments in their localities do so at their peril.

1

The Importance of Local Government and Local Elections

'The County Councillor's Song'

I am a county councillor, a very public man
To benefit the people I'll do everything I can;
In all my waking moments for their welfare I will scheme
And in the arms of Morpheus of improvements I will dream.
A local legislator and a man of high renown,
I am the county councillor, the greatest man in town

As first printed in the *Leinster Leader* newspaper, 1 May 1900.

L ocal elections in Ireland are somewhat of a mystery to the general public and are often ignored by academics.[1] A major reason for this is because the local government system itself and its structures are perceived to be complex. Many people in Ireland do not understand this system or what the local authorities actually do. It is therefore not surprising that local elections are either seen as unimportant or irrelevant. This apathy is shared by large portions of the media who opt to analyse local elections merely in the context of what they mean for national politics.

This chapter sets the scene and takes a broader perspective by asking two fundamental questions: (a) why do we need a local government system and (b) within the local government system, why are elections important?

Why do we need local government?

There is no imperative to have a local government system and yet most countries in the world choose to have one. Why is this the case? One basic reason is the building and expression of community identity. Local authorities are governments of particular communities and the institutions of local government ought to reflect and reinforce people's sense of place and community.[2] In essence, the argument is that local government is an instrument of local democracy. In its purest form, we are talking about a system whereby councils of elected politicians make policy decisions on behalf of their local communities. Powers are not retained at central level by national government but are held and maintained by the citizens of each community. Therefore, as well as local government being a means of self-expression, it also serves as a safeguard against central government domination. The spreading of power is a fundamental justification for local government, the argument being that it is dangerous to concentrate power in one organ of the state.

This is linked to the argument that the main benefit of local government is the very fact that it is *local* and therefore accessible to the general public. In fact, local government has a 'democratic primacy'[3] over central government because more people can participate in how they are governed. This promotes citizenship and encourages people to take an interest in policy choices. For example, there may be opportunities for people to participate at open public meetings, at local referenda, via interactive websites, at citizens' panels or through a local development plan process. Many non-party (Independent) candidates enter local government through community work or residents' associations and, at town council level especially, can win a seat with a couple of hundred votes. In a sense, we can also then argue that local government provides a political education for those who participate and, in many cases, local councils are used as stepping stones by candidates who, down the line, wish to pursue a career in national politics.

Local government also stresses diversity and it is often referred to as the *government of difference*. In its role as a mouthpiece of shared community interests, a local authority can factor an area's history, geography, political culture and economy into its decision-making process. Local authorities differ significantly and the needs of citizens in the Cork City Council jurisdiction will not be the same as those of the citizens in Bundoran Town Council, Donegal. As towns and communities vary in their character, it is appropriate that they are given autonomy to introduce local bye-laws that suit them best rather than the imposition of generic 'one-size-fits-all' policies. Sometimes, these local laws might appear to be eccentric but they emphasise diversity. For example, in the town of Brewerton, Alabama, the use of motorboats is forbidden on city streets; in Blythe, California, a person must own at least two cows before being permitted to wear cowboy boots in public.

Through responding to diverse circumstances, local authorities are often to the forefront of developing innovative solutions and policies that can be adapted for use elsewhere or nationally. Local government is then a laboratory of democracy[4] and this is another one of its advantages: owing to their size and accessibility local authorities can respond quickly to situations and develop innovative strategies. They can also be utilised as test case areas by central government for experimental policies.

Leaving aside democratic reasons, local government is justified on practical grounds, that is, as a provider of services locally. Whether it is in the area of water supply and sewerage or road transportation and safety, it is essential to have an organ of government that is capable of delivering these services at a local level. Of course, it can be argued that service provision could come through a system of local administration or functional decentralisation, as opposed to local *government,* but this view misses the point that locally elected representatives, with community knowledge and an understanding of the characteristics of the area, are best placed to develop strategies and provide services. Ultimately, the provision of services is the most discernible area of local government activity. Local government can also have an important role to play as an agent of central government and as a local regulator.[5] It is not unusual for central government to make use of its network of local authorities as agents. For example, in Ireland, the local authorities act as an agent of central government in collecting motor tax on behalf of the state. In areas such as planning and environmental protection, it is appropriate that local authorities play a role in ensuring that national standards are being complied with.

In summary, while the provision of public services is important, the broader justification for elected local government is on democratic and pluralist grounds. Local government is a critical element within any country's democratic system and it can act as a safeguard against central domination and absolutism by putting in place a local system of political checks and balances. In this context, local government is a guardian of basic values about the spreading of political power and is not a passing luxury.[6]

Why are local elections important?

If local government was solely limited to the provision of services to the community then elections would not be necessary as the system would, in effect, be one of local administration. The points made previously about local government expressing community identity, being mouthpieces of shared local values and acting as a counterbalance against central domination are dependent on local elections. Local elections are about deciding how our villages, towns, cities and counties are run; they are not substitute general elections. However, this is not always how local elections are regarded. For every person who casts a vote based on local issues, another person will vote on national issues or on the basis of a national popularity poll.

Local elections are exciting because of the number of individual contests involved and the diversity of candidates and issues. In June 2009, Irish residents have the opportunity to vote in 258 separate local elections to elect 1,627 local public representatives. While local elections are occasionally fought on a universal local government issue – water charges were the dominant theme in 1985 – it is more usual to find a plethora of contentious local issues such as road developments, incinerators, telephone masts, halting sites and dumps. Accordingly, single-issue, protest-based candidates appear regularly on local ballot papers. Examples in the past include Tom Gildea who was elected as a member of Donegal County Council in 1999 (following his election as an Independent TD in 1997) for his campaign to legalise deflectors that retransmitted British television channels in rural areas. In 2004, Luke Flanagan (aka 'Ming the Merciless') won a seat on Roscommon County Council by highlighting the lack of recreational facilities in the county. Previously he contested and lost six local and general elections on a platform of legalising cannabis. Luke 'Ming' Flanagan took 40 per cent of the votes in Castlerea in 2004 after an old-style election campaign in which he stood on the boot of his car and addressed mass-goers every weekend. In addition to the main political parties and Independent candidates, Ireland has had many small groups registered as political parties to contest local (and Dáil) elections. More detail on this is provided in chapter 7, but some of these include the Donegal Progressive Party and the South Kerry Independent Alliance.

Local elections are important as they provide a clear indication of the state of local government and of local democracy through measurements such as voter participation and the level of contests for seats. Ireland's turnout at local elections will be discussed later in the book but the figure of 59 per cent from the 2004 elections is reasonably healthy, especially in comparison with England where the turnout at the 2008 local elections was 35 per cent. Another area of good health for Irish local elections is that in 2004 all electoral areas were contested, that is, in every area there were more candidates than available seats. As will be discussed later, this owes much to the Irish electoral system of multi-seat constituencies.

While we mentioned above that local elections should not be regarded as substitute general elections, it cannot be denied that local contests provide important information about the broader political system. Issues that emerge on the doorstep at local level can evolve into national issues by the time of the next general election. On the basis that local and central government form part of the same governmental framework and are meant to work in partnership, this is wholly appropriate.

Local elections also play a crucial role in educating the public about local government. General knowledge about local government is already lacking but, without local election campaigns where information is supplied about the workings of the system, it would descend into total ignorance. In addition, local elections copper-fasten the link between taxation and representation, which is a core political principle, though it is one that has been weakened in Ireland

7

since the abolition of domestic rates in the late 1970s. (This is expanded on in chapter 2.)

Conclusion

Local government exists for two essential reasons: as a manifestation of local democracy and as a provider of local public services. Both are important and the holding of regular, well-contested, local elections is the primary route for citizen participation and the articulation of community values. Ireland's local authorities and the services they provide 'have a far more immediate, continuous and comprehensive impact on all of our daily lives'[7] than many of the issues which dominate national headlines. In the next chapter we will examine the Irish local government system and assess its strengths and weaknesses.

2

The Irish Local Government System

The aim of this chapter is to describe the local government system that exists in Ireland because the institutional context is an important factor in local elections. Elected councillors are the supreme decision-makers in any local authority and many candidates go forward for election with a general commitment to serve the community. As laudable as this motivation may be, candidates often have no idea what this service involves. Being a councillor must be the only position in local government that does not come with a job description and councillors tend to discover how the local government system operates during – rather than before – their term in office. This chapter presents and assesses the local government system, from its formal beginnings in 1898 to the present day. For existing and prospective local elected representatives, knowledge of this system is paramount to their success as a councillor.

Overview

There are 114 local authorities in the Republic of Ireland, divided between county councils (29), city councils (5), borough councils (5) and town councils (75). The primary focus of this book is on local elections at the county and city levels, that is, Ireland's thirty-four principal local government units. While it might be anticipated that Ireland would have twenty-six county councils – based on one per county – the position is that Dublin County Council was abolished via the Local Government (Dublin) Act, 1993, and replaced with three separate authorities: Dún Laoghaire–Rathdown, Fingal and South Dublin. Also, dating back to a division in 1838, Tipperary forms two county councils, North Tipperary and South Tipperary. Hence, we have a total of twenty-nine county councils. City councils (called city corporations until the Local Government Act, 2001) exist in Cork, Dublin, Limerick, Galway and Waterford.

Apart from Dáil Éireann and the presidency, local government is the only Irish institution whose members are directly elected by all of the people. Accordingly, local government has both a representational and operational role. Local elections take place every five years. The scheduling of local elections has only recently been guaranteed by Article 28A of the Irish constitution (passed by referendum in 1999), which requires that elections are held no later than the end of the fifth year after which they were last held. Electors vote for councillors by secret ballot on the principle of proportional representation with the single transferable vote (PR-STV). Between the 114 local councils, there are a total of 1,627 councillors with 883 at county and city level and 744 at town and borough level. Voter turnout at the 2004 local elections was 59 per cent, an increase of eight percentage points from the previous round.

The elected council is formally the policy-making arm of the local authority with responsibility for the adoption of annual budgets, bye-laws and development plans. The daily management of the local authority is the remit of a full-time chief executive, referred to as the county or city manager. The manager runs the local authority within the parameters laid down by the elected members. Legally, any function that is not specified in legislation as a policy function for the members becomes the responsibility of the manager.

Local authorities in Ireland undertake a variety of functions, which are typically divided into the following eight categories:

- Housing and Building
- Road Transportation and Safety
- Water Supply and Sewerage
- Development Incentives and Control
- Environmental Protection
- Recreation and Amenities
- Agriculture, Education, Health and Welfare
- Miscellaneous

While the above list might appear broad, the reality is that local authorities in Ireland have a very narrow range of functions in comparison to most other European countries. The Irish system reflects a top-down approach 'with specific functions being allocated by central government, which exercises control'.[1] For example, 'education' might seem an important local government function but the main role for local councils in education is the administration of grants on behalf of the Higher Education Authority (HEA).

Irish local government is funded through a combination of commercial rates, charges for goods and services, and transfers from central government. A major review of financing was conducted by Indecon International Economic Consultants in 2005, which concluded that local government in Ireland was characterised by vertical imbalance, with a high degree of centralisation in funding provision.[2] The Indecon Report highlighted that in 2004, 56 per cent of local government funding was locally based (31 per cent from charges for goods and services and 25 per cent from commercial rates) with 44 per cent coming directly from central government in the form of grants and subsidies. A more recent report from the Organisation for Economic Co-Operation and Development (OECD) in April 2008 states that the balance has shifted with 52 per cent of local authority funding being provided by central government. The OECD report also draws attention to the fact that 'from an international perspective, there is little fiscal autonomy in Ireland'.[3] As providers of services and purchasers of goods and services, Irish local authorities are a substantial element of the economy; in 2007, councils spent €10 billion, with 45 per cent on current expenditure and 55 per cent on capital expenditure.

The Department of the Environment, Heritage and Local Government oversees the local government system and implements policy with regard to local government functions, financing and structures. John Gormley TD (leader of the Green Party) was appointed Minister for the Environment, Heritage and Local Government in 2007 and he launched a Green Paper in April 2008 with the primary aim of renewing local democratic leadership and strengthening local democracy. The Green Paper proposes the introduction of a regional mayor for Dublin, elected directly by the people of Dublin, with strategic functions including planning, housing, waste, water provision and waste-water disposal.

History (Pre-1898)

The earliest territorial reference in Ireland is the 'tuath', which became recognised as the 'county' at the end of the twelfth century under the reign of King John. A sheriff, appointed by the king, controlled each county and he was an important person with many powers, including committing people to prison. The Normans had introduced the Grand Jury system earlier in the twelfth century, and it was the sheriff who took responsibility for selecting the Jury members. Grand Juries were the original county councils and they assumed more powers and functions over time. Initially, they only convened twice yearly for baronial presentment sessions but, from the seventeenth century, assumed administrative functions. This involved the Grand Jury system being used for the construction of roads, for police work and the erecting and financing of new county infirmaries.[4]

In terms of urban government, the Anglo-Norman model of establishing a network of municipalities was employed with towns granted royal charters for self-government. In the seventeenth century, the Stuart kings set up corporations, the existence of which was decidedly undemocratic: 'by the time of the Union in 1800, most corporations bore a closer resemblance to exclusive clubs, with membership often restricted to individuals drawn from a single family, than to governing bodies'.[5] Municipal reform commenced in piece-meal fashion with the Lighting of Towns Act, 1828 (creating town commissioners), the Reform Act of 1832 and the Towns Improvement (Ireland) Act, 1854. However, the distinguishing feature of urban local government largely remained in the way that 'civic authority was centralised in self-perpetuating oligarchies'.[6]

The situation in rural Ireland was little better, with power vested in a landed elite whose members often regarded local government as a source of personal status and influence, not as a civic responsibility.[7] The Irish Poor Law system developed in tandem with the Grand Juries. While in England poor relief was provided for in the Elizabethan Act of 1601, the earliest Poor Law act in Ireland was not passed until 1771. The principal enactment, though, was the Irish Poor Relief Act, 1838, which followed from the investigations of a special commission – the Irish Poor Inquiry. The importance of the 1838 act is that it introduced two significant elements into Irish local government – limited representation of the people and central control. Poor Law boards were created to administer poor relief as the country was divided into unions. Relief in each union was provided by the boards (referred to as either Poor Law Boards or Boards of Guardians), which in turn were under the control of the Dublin-based Poor Law Commissioners. The Boards of Guardians were the first representative local bodies in Ireland but were only part elected. Typically, power was vested in landowners while there were also ex-officio members, examples being justices of the peace. By 1851 there were 130 Poor Law unions in the country and the Boards of Guardians were soon granted extra powers with regard to health and the dispensary system by the Medical Charities Act, 1851.

The expansion of the Poor Law system, side by side with an increasingly unsatisfactory Grand Jury regime led to confusion and a Frankenstein's-monster patchwork of overlapping authorities and jurisdictions.[8] From the mid-nineteenth century it was apparent that reform of the local government system could not be avoided as abuse of powers, partiality and blatant corruption were its primary characteristics. There were some half-hearted reform attempts but the Home Rule struggle was the most pressing issue at the time and in the build-up to the landmark 1898 act, local administration was in chaos.

Local Government (Ireland) Act, 1898

The primary purpose of the act of 1898 was to put county government on a representative basis. The landed gentry were to lose their absolute power over local administration but their loss was tempered by a shrewd financial arrangement under which landlords were relieved of half their poor rate liability. The act met with very little opposition in parliament as unionists viewed local government reform as a more favourable alternative to Home Rule. While the act of 1898 is arguably the most significant piece of legislation in the history of Irish local government, it can be seen that the structure that emerged was not radically different from what had existed previously – rather, the membership was changed fundamentally.

The main effects of the 1898 legislation became apparent the following year when the first elections were held. Landlords virtually disappeared from the system as new representatives entered the local government arena. A noteworthy feature of the 1899 elections was the smooth changeover to the new system of local government and the increased representation due to the broadening of the franchise, 'a tribute to the democratic spirit prevailing in Ireland'.[9] Interestingly, this contrasts with the pre-1898 mood as 'democratic local government, of which county councils were the central example, was a virtually unwanted gift from the Conservative government to the Irish people. There was no agitation in its favour'.[10] Another legacy of the Local Government (Ireland) Act, 1898 is that the system changed from a haphazard, landlord-dominated environment to one in which legislation became more frequent and complex and the need for officials and bureaucratic rules gained prominence.

Turmoil and Change, 1899–1922

The period from the late nineteenth century to 1922 (when Ireland gained independence) has been described as 'one of spasmodic disintegration of British rule in Ireland, of increasing confusion, inefficiency and petty corruption, culminating in the breakdown of law and order'.[11] At the turn of the nineteenth century, Ireland's local government system closely resembled its counterparts in England and Wales with close to 600 local authorities of all kinds, including county councils and rural district councils. The final piece of British legislation on local administration in Ireland was the Local Government (Ireland) Act, 1919, which made proportional representation the voting mechanism in local elections. In 1920, Dáil Éireann established a local government department under Minister W. T. Cosgrave in 'competition' with the Local Government Board (LGB), which had been set up in 1872 and was based in the Custom House. Most local authorities supported the fledgling department but, for a short while, there were two central authorities in existence. The LGB announced that annual grants-in-aid paid to local councils would be withheld unless the local authorities accepted the authority of the British government. While the majority of local authorities broke off all contact with the LGB, others such as Dublin Corporation and Kilkenny County Council continued to recognise both sides, much to the annoyance of Cosgrave.

In May 1921, the Custom House was destroyed by the IRA and all of its records were lost. Later in the year a truce was called, which paved the way for the Anglo-Irish Treaty, signed in London on 6 December before being approved by the Dáil on 7 January 1922. The Treaty stated that the Irish Free State, comprising twenty-six counties, would be a dominion of the British Empire. The new government wasted no time in getting down to business and created the Department of Local Government.

Retrenchment, 1923–1940

An early legislative measure of the new parliament was the Local Government (Temporary Provisions) Act, 1923, which effectively abolished the lingering Boards of Guardians and placed the administration of Poor Law on a county basis. It also provided for the dissolution of local authorities that were not performing their functions and their replacement by commissioners. This was followed by the Local Government Act, 1925, which abolished the rural district councils and greatly reduced the number of locally elected bodies in the system. Local government commentators have cited this particular piece of legislation as influential in the creation of a centralised mentality and there is no doubt that this was a period of retrenchment in which local government was emasculated.[12] It should be observed, however, that Ireland at that time had been through a period of enormous turbulence, with the battle for independence from Britain followed by a bitter civil war. A tight rein with strict centralised control was deemed appropriate for a small, divided country with a new government seeking authority and respect. Essentially, the needs of the time ensured a substantial intrusion by the central administration into local government and centralism became an accepted facet of government in Ireland.

Since 1925 the system of local government in Ireland has developed at a leisurely pace and the basic structures have remained virtually unaltered. The management system has been the most significant advance and it emerged following the regular use by the Minister for Local Government of the power of dissolution, 'which was used freely at first, and with breathtaking disregard of the antiquity and prestige of the victims. Whether dissolution was a deserved or appropriate fate is debatable, but the surprising thing was the quiet acquiescence of the citizens in these violent assaults on their civic privileges, such as they were'.[13]

Twenty-three bodies were dissolved because of political dissent or financial problems and replaced by commissioners within the first three years of the 1923 act. The Kerry and Leitrim County Councils have the dubious distinction of being the first two authorities to be dissolved (in May 1923) while other victims include Dublin Corporation (May 1924) and Cork Corporation (October 1924). The decision to dissolve Cork Corporation 'was a political one which maintained the trend towards centralisation and the loss of local autonomy'.[14] The dissolution mechanism was originally designed as a temporary, punitive measure to punish troublesome local authorities. However, the commissioners soon began to have a positive influence on local administration. Their reliability and administrative competence (the early commissioners typically were senior civil servants from the Department of Local Government) earned them praise and respect from both central government and the local electorate. The concept of administrative rule developed and a strong supporting lobby group emerged in Cork city, with commercial and industrial interests to the fore. Despite strong opposition, the Cork City Management Act, 1929 was passed with a permanent official, Philip Monahan, sharing power with (rather than replacing) the elected representatives. Monahan retained his post as city manager in Cork until 1959 and he essentially defined the local authority management system. Dublin and Dún Laoghaire (1930), Limerick (1934) and Waterford (1939) adopted the Cork model and the system was finally extended to the entire country with the County Management Act, 1940. To the present day, it is this power-sharing relationship between management and elected members that is at the heart of understanding local government in Ireland.

Intense Centralisation, 1941–1957

By the 1940s, 'intense centralisation and general subordination to central government' were the dominant themes in local government.[15] The 1940s and 1950s were largely uneventful decades in the local government arena but two developments warrant a mention in the context of local elections. In 1947, a government bill to make the local electoral system less proportional was passed in the Dáil and Seanad but it did not become law due to technical reasons. While this bill did not propose removing proportional representation for parliamentary elections, the government sought to introduce single-member electoral areas in the counties. In addition, it was proposed that urban areas would be separately represented on the county council. Speaking at the second stage debate in the Dáil on 26 November 1947, Minister Seán MacEntee noted:

> [...] the Bill seeks to reimpose upon the members of county councils that peculiar personal obligation which attaches to a single individual who does not

share with others the responsibility of representing a particular district. [...] The fact that the single-member system of proportional representation, while quite unsuitable for the Legislature, is almost ideal for electing a local authority, arises from the fundamental difference between the National Assembly and a local authority. [...] A local authority is an entirely subordinate body and can only exercise such powers and perform such duties as may be delegated to it by the Oireachtas. [...] The primary purpose of a local authority is in fact administrative. [...] In order that this may be done effectively, it is highly desirable, if not indeed essential, that the local authority shall be equally as representative of all parts of the area which it administers, as it is of the area as a whole. Equal distribution of representation, however, can only be attained when each individual member is specifically elected to represent a particular area (Dáil debates Vol. 109, col. 42).

Although the legislation changing to single member electoral areas for local elections never saw the light of day, it would have radically altered the system of local government had it gone through. What is very clear from the above quote was MacEntee's belief in local administration as opposed to local government. There is a tendency for all Irish political parties to champion the cause of local democracy while in opposition but, in office, to display centralist tendencies.[16] The other significant development came in 1953 when the time period for the holding of local elections was extended from three years to five years.

From Optimism to Financial Hardship, 1958–1990

The 1960s brought prosperity and optimism on the back of the 1958 Programme for Economic Expansion (the first national strategy in Ireland and the first attempt at economic planning). The positive mood was reflected in the Local Government (Planning and Development) Act, 1963, which envisaged local authorities expanding their roles into 'development corporations'. The optimism soon dissipated and the potential of local government at this time was never realised, partly because 'arteries had grown too hard and bureaucratic sclerosis had become too far advanced'.[17]

The following decade saw local authorities relieved of their health functions (with the establishment of regional health boards) and also relieved of financial independence. An auction between the main political parties before the 1977 general election resulted in the abolition of rates on domestic dwellings (the primary source of local authority funding) on the basis that the exchequer would meet the costs. The Local Government (Financial Provisions) Act, 1978 – which gave effect to the abolition of domestic rates – has had a hugely negative impact on local government finance. It has interfered with the local democratic process, curtailed local accountability, weakened local discretion, reduced the amount of money available to local authorities and made local government more dependent on central government'.[18] Initially, the government paid the local authorities a support grant in lieu of the domestic rate monies but in 1983 legislation removed responsibility from the minister to meet the full amount of money lost. Rates on agricultural land were subsequently removed in 1984 following a Supreme Court case, which ruled that the use of the valuation system as a basis for levying rates was unconstitutional. The loss of rates as a source of finance has severely restricted local authorities to the present time.

Reform and Modernisation Efforts, 1991–2009

The 1990s saw various reform efforts, with minimal impact on the overall structure or operations of the local government system. The Local Government Act, 1991 relaxed the *ultra vires* doctrine (which stated that local authorities could not go beyond their statutory powers) and enhanced the socio-economic role of authorities. This legislation also paved the way for the establishment of eight regional authorities with responsibility for the co-ordination of local authority activity. The following two years saw the creation of the Environmental Protection Agency (EPA) and the National Roads Authority (NRA). Both are specialised central agencies, which have assumed powers formerly exercised by local authorities.

The mid-1990s saw a burst of activity and plenty of reports into local government. The Fine Gael, Labour Party and Democratic Left coalition government that came to power in 1994 made a commitment to reform local government and set about analysing the system under the headings of functions, form and finance. A Devolution Commission was formed in 1995 and produced an interim and second report over the next two years recommending functions that could be devolved to the local level. The

23

question of form, or structure, was left to a Reorganisation Commission, which reported (*Towards Cohesive Local Government – Town and County*) in 1996. Amongst other things, it recommended a single classification of town authorities, all to be titled town councils with an office of mayor. KPMG Consultants produced a report *The Financing of Local Government in Ireland* in the same year. The report claimed that the Irish system was too highly centralised, had limited discretion, too narrow a base and no natural buoyancy.[19]

The individual reports into functions, form and finance combined into a government strategy document *Better Local Government – A Programme for Change,* which was published in December 1996. *Better Local Government* (BLG) originated in the wider public service reform programme, the Strategic Management Initiative, which, in turn, can be located within the global New Public Management (NPM) movement. BLG contains four core principles:

- Enhancing local democracy
- Serving the customer better
- Developing efficiency
- Providing proper resources for local authorities

The primary initial output from BLG was the establishment of strategic policy committees (SPCs) and corporate policy groups (CPGs) to involve councillors more in policy development in partnership with local communities and external interests. The SPC system has been a limited success to date with significant variances in effectiveness across the country.

The next major development was the Local Government Act, 2001, which legislated for some of the recommendations contained in BLG. The 2001 act was heralded in advance by the then Minister of the Environment and Local Government, Noel Dempsey, as the greatest shake-up of local government in the history of the state. It codified existing local government legislation; re-named authorities as county councils, city councils and town councils; created a general ethics framework for councillors and staff; allowed for the establishment of a Boundary Commission; put SPCs on a statutory footing and introduced a representational payment for councillors. The legislation also sparked debates on three significant issues. First, the decision to transfer water and sanitary functions from town to county authorities brought into sharp focus the concept of achieving economies of scale while eroding local democracy and contradicting the principle of subsidiarity.[20] Secondly, the Local Government Act, 2001 maintained the status of the dual mandate (whereby elected members could simultaneously hold local authority and Oireachtas seats) despite the provision in the Local Government Bill, 2000 that the dual mandate would be abolished. The third major issue was that the legislation proposed, from 2004, the direct election of mayors who would have executive functions.

Noel Dempsey's claims for the 2001 act were weakened by the fact that his immediate successor in the Custom House, Martin Cullen, wasted no time in reversing two of the key elements of the legislation. Under Cullen's Local Government Act, 2003, the dual mandate was abolished and the proposed direct election of mayors was scrapped. In

2004, Minister Cullen launched an initiative aimed at extending public accountability in the local government sector through the introduction of service indicators. *Delivering Value for People – Service Indicators in Local Authorities* put forward forty-two indicators under which the performance of local councils would be assessed. Examples of the indicators are:

- Percentage and tonnage of household waste recycled
- Speed with which local authority housing units are filled
- Time taken to determine planning applications
- Library opening hours
- Rates collected

The list of forty-two indicators emerged from a working party comprising six high-ranking local government officials, civil servants in the Department of the Environment, Heritage and Local Government and a representative from the Institute of Public Administration but no members of the public or elected representatives were invited to sit on the committee. Each summer the Local Government Management Services Board (LGMSB) reports to the Minister for the Environment, Heritage and Local Government on the performance of the local authorities across the range of indicators for the previous calendar year. As acknowledged by the most recent LGMSB report, the forty-two service indicators used to evaluate Irish local authorities do not capture the full picture of local government activity. Indicators do have a value – albeit a limited one – in presenting a view of performance over time and allowing individual local authorities to chart their progress (or otherwise) on a yearly basis. Service indicators are just that: a useful tool to indicate to the local authority how it is performing and if there are problem areas that need to be addressed. The data produced is not an end in itself, but a stepping stone to improved service delivery.

Also in 2004, the minister commissioned Indecon International Economic Consultants to conduct an independent review of local government financing in Ireland. As previously mentioned (see overview), the Indecon Report of 2005 highlighted vertical imbalance and a high degree of centralisation. In recommending more locally based sources of funding, the report stated that simply to maintain service provision at 2004 levels, additional expenditure in the order of €1,000 to €2,000 million per annum would be required by 2010. Indecon, furthermore, proposed the extension of water charges to non-principal private dwellings in the context that local authorities should charge full economic costs of providing services on behalf of central government. As always, any proposed local charge or taxation will be politically sensitive and the fear is that – in the absence of strong government policy to enhance local government finance – local authorities will face crippling income problems into the future. With this in mind, the rejection by the Department of the Environment, Heritage and Local Government of the major recommendations of the Indecon Report has disheartened those anticipating genuine reform.

In April 2008 the eagerly awaited OECD report on the Irish public service was published. *Ireland: Towards an Integrated Public Service* highlights that 'Ireland has limited local autonomy which, in turn, strengthens the input-focus of national policies'.[21] At a more general level, the OECD criticises the focus of the Irish public service on performance reporting rather than performance managing, a comment which can be applied to the use of service indicators in local government. In the wake of the OECD report, the government established a task force on public service, which produced *Transforming Public Services: Citizen Centred – Performance Focused*. The secretary general at the Department of the Environment, Heritage and Local Government sat on the Task Force and local councillors as well as city and county managers were amongst the stakeholders interviewed. The report follows the key themes of the OECD review and presents a number of challenges and opportunities for local government, including the following:

- Greater collaboration between national and local government
- Enhanced interaction between local authorities and other parts of the public service
- Case-based approach to deepen citizen engagement
- Local authorities to take the lead role in shared service provision
- Integrated approach in responding to the needs of particular individuals or disadvantaged groups
- Services to be delivered along county lines, or groups of counties
- Database of all publicly-funded projects to be maintained at county level to avoid duplication
- Devolution of functions from central government and agencies to the local level

- Creation of a coherent rolling programme of e-government projects
- Increased provision of online services
- Linkages between performance management systems and promotion and increments to be strengthened
- Standardisation of evaluation and assessment systems

The content and tone of both the OECD review and the task force report suggests that 'local government is slowly moving centre-stage in government thinking in terms of how public services need to be reformed and reorganised'.[22] The current programme for government produced by Fianna Fáil, the Green Party and the Progressive Democrats pledges to introduce a directly elected mayor for Dublin with executive powers by 2011. This pledge was reinforced by a Green Paper entitled *Stronger Local Democracy – Options for Change* published in April 2008. The Green Paper promotes a regional mayor for Dublin on the basis of increased visibility, the potential for enhancing democratic participation and active citizenship. Legislation governing the direct election of mayors was proposed for 2009 outlining 'what the precise functions of the mayor will be and how the office will impinge on the role currently played by the city/county manager'.[23] The principle of directly electing mayors is sound but the devil is in the detail and unless the legislation clearly outlines the division of executive powers with the manager, there is a danger that the office of mayor will be an empty role.

Conclusion

This chapter has provided the history, context and structure of local government in Ireland as well as drawing attention to recent reports and ongoing issues. It is clear that elements of the Irish local government system need urgent reform. The introduction of directly elected mayors can be regarded as one element of the reform process but the starting point must be the devolution of powers and financial autonomy from central government to local authorities. The next chapter describes how local elections operate within this system.

3

Local Elections: The Rules of the Game

The purpose of this chapter is to explain how local government elections in Ireland are organised and how they are run. Who is entitled to stand for election? Is everyone able to vote? The voting system for local elections is PR-STV and the intricacies of this system are explained by way of an example from the 2004 elections. It is important that every local election candidate knows the rules of the game and is aware of new government policies or legislative changes. For example, spending limits were introduced for the first time in 2009 and came into force for the June 2009 local elections.

Overview

The June 2009 local elections were the twenty-third to be held in Ireland. The first elections were held in April 1899, following on from the landmark Local Government (Ireland)

Act, 1898. Before 1898, Irish local government was unrepresentative, inefficient and corrupt. The system, as already described, was dominated by large landowners who sat on local Grand Juries. Any examination of local administration in the latter stages of the nineteenth century suggests a confusing array of local bodies and jurisdictions with Grand Juries, presentment sessions, Boards of Guardians, Poor Law unions and asylum districts.

The first step in bringing order to the system was the Local Government (Ireland) Act, 1898. Grand Juries were replaced by county, urban and rural district councils elected on a wide franchise that included women. The primary purpose of the legislation was to bring democracy down to the smallest community unit practicable, a shift to the democracy of farmers, shopkeepers and publicans.[1]

The act of 1898 was not especially well received by the Irish public who longed for home rule. In some quarters, it was 'met with suspicion and grudging acceptance'.[2] The first elections took place on 6 April 1899 with adverse weather conditions affecting the turnout. Polling stations were open from 8 a.m. to 8 p.m. in urban areas and 10 a.m. to 8 p.m. in rural districts. Election day passed off without many incidents although 'there were frequent comments on the level of illiteracy displayed by voters'.[3] According to *The Irish Times* of 7 April 1899, 'there was an absence of any keen excitement and the proceedings were generally characterised by good order and tranquillity'.

When it came to the first meetings of the new local authorities there was increased interest. Cork County Council convened on Saturday 22 April and 'the doors were thrown open at a quarter to twelve, when there was a rush for seats in the public gallery, which, when the business had commenced, was thronged to inconvenience'.[4] Diarmaid Ferriter's examination of newspaper reporting in the lead-up to election day and the initial meetings reveals 'a curious mixture of excitement, indifference and aggression as well as a fair share of puzzlement, ignorance and sheer bewilderment'.[5]

When must local elections be held?

The act of 1898 stated that councillors would hold office for a term of three years, and then retire together, with their places being filled via a new election. This changed in 1953 when legislation provided for the holding of elections every fifth year. However, postponement of local elections has become the norm with a minority of elections taking place according to their original schedule.[6] In all, local elections have been postponed on fifteen occasions since 1923. While the reason given for postponement in most cases has been a proposed restructuring of local government, this has never materialised to any significant extent. Prior to 1973, amending legislation was required to postpone local elections; between 1973 and 1994 it was possible to postpone elections by order of the minister (if confirmed by resolution by both Houses of the Oireachtas). The Local Government Act, 1994 reverted back to the pre-1973 position of amending legislation. The lack of respect shown by central government towards local government elections reached a peak in the 1990s as the county and city council elections scheduled for 1996 did not take place until 1999.

In 1999 the government followed through on a commitment made in the 1996 policy document, *Better Local Government – A Programme for* Change, to give constitutional recognition to local government and to local elections. In conjunction with local and European Parliament elections, a constitutional referendum was held on 11 June 1999 and an overwhelming majority of people (78 per cent) voted in favour of including a new article (28A) on local government in the constitution. In the 100-year history of Irish local government, this was a significant moment as it represented the first explicit mention of local government in the constitution. Prior to 1999, the only reference to local government in the constitution was a secondary one regarding provisions for nominating candidates for the presidency.

Article 28A (3) now clearly states that 'Elections for members of such local authorities shall be held in accordance with law not later than the end of the fifth year after the year in which they were last held'.

The policy of successive governments casually postponing local elections on a whim should now be at an end.

The Rules of Local Elections

The act of 1898 (section 1, sub-section 2) stated that the local government electorate consisted of 'all Parliamentary electors and of all peers and women who, but for being peers or women, would be entitled to be Parliamentary electors'. Though female suffrage was limited, it is telling that women were included as a feature of the new local electorate. The number of local electors in 1899, when the first elections were held, was 891,000: approximately 35 per cent of the total adult population.[7] Under the terms of the 1898 legislation, each registered elector was to have one vote, with elections to take place every three years using the simple majority voting system.

Though women could become Poor Law guardians and district councillors, they were debarred from contesting county council elections until the Local Authorities (Ireland) (Qualification of Women) Act, 1911. The ensuing stage in enfranchisement was reached in 1918 when married women aged thirty and over got the vote.

In 1898 every local government elector was eligible for the position of county councillor although the following classes of people were disqualified:

- A county coroner in the county for which she or he was the coroner
- Clergymen and regular ministers of any religious denomination
- Women
- An infant or alien
- Anyone who had received union relief within twelve months of the election
- Anyone who had been convicted of any crime within five years of the election
- Anyone who had been declared bankrupt within five years of the election
- Anyone who held a paid office or place of profit under the council

- Anyone who participated in the profit of a contract with the council

The act placed no limits on the amount of money that a candidate could spend in contesting a local election.

The Local Government Acts of 2001 and 2003, as well as the Electoral Amendment Acts of 2001, 2002 and 2006 set out the current local electoral rules but between 1898 and the present day there have often been changes to the system, the most important of which are highlighted below.

1911 – Women were allowed to contest county council elections.

1918 – Married women over thirty years of age got the right to vote in local elections.

1919 – Proportional representation was introduced, on an experimental basis, in the Sligo municipal borough and was generally implemented for local elections in 1920.

1923 – The power of dissolution was introduced (see chapter 2).

1929 – The Cork City Management Act was passed (see chapter 2).

1935 – Universal suffrage for local elections was introduced.

1940 – The Cork city management system was extended to all counties.

1953 – The time period for the holding of local elections was extended from three years to five years.

1963 – Responsibility for the registration of electors was transferred to the county councils.

1974 – Legislation relating to the questioning of a local election result by means of an election petition was passed.

1991 – Members of parliament who became ministers or minsters of state were barred from holding a local authority seat.

1994 – Legislation banned Oireachtas and European Parliament members from holding the chair or mayoralty on local authorities from 1999.

1999 – An amendment to the constitution was passed, safeguarding the holding of local elections every five years.

2001 – The legislation governing local government elections was updated.

2003 – The dual mandate was abolished, prohibiting the simultaneous holding of a local government seat with an Oireachtas seat.

2008 – The Electoral (Amendment) Bill was published in June. The purpose of the Bill was to amend the law relating to the Constituency Commission and to provide revised alternative procedures for nomination of non-party candidates at European and local elections. Also, as a result of the Electoral Boundary Report 2008, the number of Local Electoral Areas in Dublin was reduced from 13 to 11, bringing the national total to 258.

2009 – Local election spending limits were introduced, ranging from €15,000 to €7,500 (covered later in chapter).

The current position

Part four of the Local Government Act, 2001 sets out the law governing the conduct of local elections, in conjunction with the Local Election Regulations, 1995. The 2001 act is noteworthy as it codifies and updates all previous local government legislation. Voting at local elections is open to citizens of any state, but they must be over eighteen years of age, ordinarily resident in Ireland and on the register of electors compiled annually by the county and city councils. Inclusion on the electoral register requires the completion of an application form returned to the local authority where resident. It is not permissible to vote in both a county council and city council election, but one can vote in a borough or town council election in addition to the county council level. In November 2007 Minister Gormley launched a public information campaign to promote awareness of the register of electors. Voters can now check if they are on the register by contacting their local authority or by going online to www.checktheregister.ie. The Department of the Environment, Heritage and Local Government website, www.environ.ie, contains information on the register of electors in Latvian, Lithuanian, Mandarin, Polish, Romanian, Russian and Slovak.

Contesting local elections is an open process and, as with voting, is not restricted to Irish citizens. The main criteria are that candidates must be ordinarily resident in Ireland and must be over eighteen years of age. Under sections 12 and 13 of the Local Government Act, 2001, the following people are disqualified from seeking local authority membership:

- A member of the European Commission, Parliament or Courts
- A Minister of the Government or a Minister of State
- An Ceann Comhairle (the Chairman of the Dáil) and an Cathaoirleach (the Chairman of the Seanad)
- Members of An Garda Síochána or a full-time member of the Irish defence forces
- Judges
- The Comptroller and Auditor General
- Civil servants who are not – by the terms of their employment – expressly permitted to be a member of a local authority
- Those who have been imprisoned for a term longer than six months
- Those who have failed to pay local authority charges
- Local authority employees (certain grades are exempted from this disqualification under section 161 of the 2001 Act)
- Those who have failed to comply with an order of a court to pay money due to a local authority
- Those who have been convicted of fraud or dishonest dealings, corrupt practice or acting while disqualified

Another disqualification was subsequently introduced through the Local Government (No. 2) Act, 2003 which prohibited Oireachtas members from local authority membership from the 2004 local elections onwards. This 'double jobbing' at national and local level, commonly referred to as the dual mandate, has been a significant feature of Irish political life. For example, of the 226 members elected to the Dáil or Seanad in 2002, 138 were also members of local councils (see chapter 7).

Local electoral areas and nominations

A local electoral area (LEA) is a constituency for the purpose of a local authority election. Every city and county is divided into a number of LEAs, varying from three to thirteen, by order of the Minister for the Environment, Heritage and Local Government under section 23 of the 2001 legislation. The number of members of each local authority is fixed by schedule 7 of the act, as follows:

TABLE 3.1 NUMBER OF MEMBERS OF EACH COUNTY AND CITY COUNCIL

County Councils	Number of Members
Carlow	21
Cavan	25
Clare	32
Cork	48
Donegal	29
Dún Laoghaire–Rathdown	28
Fingal	24
Galway	30
Kerry	27
Kildare	25
Kilkenny	26
Laois	25
Leitrim	22
Limerick	28
Longford	21
Louth	26
Mayo	31
Meath	29

⟶

Monaghan	20
North Tipperary	21
Offaly	21
Roscommon	26
Sligo	25
South Dublin	26
South Tipperary	26
Waterford	23
Westmeath	23
Wexford	21
Wicklow	24
Total	**753**

City Councils	Number of Members
Cork	31
Dublin	52
Galway	15
Limerick	17
Waterford	15
Total	**130**

As can be seen from the above tables, the two largest local authorities in Ireland (at least in terms of membership) are Dublin City Council with fifty-two and Cork County Council with forty-eight. Although not detailed above, the five borough councils of Clonmel, Drogheda, Kilkenny, Sligo and Wexford have twelve members apiece. Nine members is the norm in the majority of town councils, the exceptions being Bray, Dundalk and Tralee which have twelve each.

County and city councils may apply to the minister, after public consultation, for a change in their membership totals.

Equally, town councils with a population in excess of 15,000 people may seek an increase from nine to twelve members. There is no constitutional or statutory requirement regarding councillor/population ratios between different counties and cities and they vary widely.[8]

While we think of local elections in terms of securing members for a network of 114 local authorities, the truth of the matter is that 258 individual elections take place across the country's LEAs. For example, if we look at Roscommon County Council, which has twenty-six elected councillors, we can see that it is divided into six distinct LEAs – Athlone (5), Ballaghaderreen (4), Boyle (5), Castlerea (3), Roscommon (5) and Strokestown (4).

A period of one week for nominating candidates to run for election occurs four weeks before polling day. A person may nominate themselves or consent to be nominated by an elector registered in the local area. It is possible that a person can be nominated to stand in more than one area. The nomination form of a candidate from a political party must have a certificate of political affiliation attached. A non-party candidate is required by law (section 3 of the Electoral Amendment Act, 2002) to have her or his form assented to by fifteen electors from the LEA (Electoral Amendment Bill, 2008). The fifteen signatures cannot include the candidate or any proposer. If the candidate has no party affiliation, the person may be described as 'non-party' or may choose to leave the appropriate space blank on the nomination form. The candidate or proposer is responsible for ensuring that the completed nomination paper is delivered to the local authority returning officer before the closing date (typically mid-May). The returning officer must rule on the validity of a nomination paper within one hour of its presentation.

Organisation of the election

Much of the information which follows is drawn from the document 'How Members of Local Authorities are Elected' which can be downloaded from the Department of the Environment, Heritage and Local Government website. As previously mentioned, local elections now take place every five years in the month of June. The polling day is fixed by the respective minister and she or he also specifies the precise polling period which must be at least twelve hours between 7.00 a.m. and 10.30 p.m. It is required that polling takes place on the same day throughout the country, except in the case of on islands if the returning officer deems that polling should take place in advance, owing to weather or transport problems. As with national elections, postal voting is permitted at the local level and special arrangements are put in place for voters resident in hospitals or similar institutions.

The responsibility for conducting the election to each council rests with the local authority returning officer and all costs associated with running the election are met by the local council. Not all elections are necessarily contested: for example, in 1999 a poll was not required in two LEAs as the number of candidates equalled the number of available seats. One of the areas was Kilbeggan, Westmeath, where there were only four candidates declared for the four available seats. Due to his alphabetical ranking, Fianna Fáil's Tom

Cowley became the first councillor elected in the country during the 1999 election. Similarly, in 1999, the nine candidates for Loughrea Town Commission (now Loughrea Town Council) were deemed elected without a contest. This is an unusual occurrence where there are multi-seat constituencies and it more commonly arises in the context of a first-past-the-post electoral system. At the 2004 local elections, eight candidates contested the four seats in the Kilbeggan LEA and fourteen candidates went forward for the nine vacancies on Loughrea Town Council.

On polling day electors may be required to produce evidence of identity such as a passport, a marriage certificate or a driving licence. Electors vote in secret in a voting compartment on a ballot paper containing the names of the candidates in alphabetical order, their photograph, political affiliation and party emblem, if any. The voter indicates the order of their choice by writing 1 opposite their first choice, 2 opposite their second choice and so on.

The count

The counting of votes begins at 9 a.m. on the day after polling. By this stage, all ballot boxes will have been taken to a central counting place for each local authority. Every box is opened and the number of ballot papers checked against the return provided by each presiding officer. They are then thoroughly mixed and sorted according to the first preferences recorded for each candidate, with invalid papers being rejected. The PR-STV electoral system is based on the principle of a quota, which is the minimum number of votes necessary to guarantee the election of a candidate. The quota is calculated by dividing the total number of valid ballot papers by one more than the number of seats to be filled and adding one to the result. So, in a three-seat LEA where the valid poll was 8,568 votes, the quota is 8,568 divided by $(3 + 1) + 1 = 2,143$.

At the end of the first count any candidate who has received a number of votes equal to or greater than the quota is deemed to be elected. If a candidate receives more than the quota, the surplus votes are transferred proportionately to the remaining candidates in the following way: if the candidate's votes are all first preference votes, her or his entire ballot papers are sorted into separate parcels according to the next preference shown on them. A separate parcel is made of the non-transferable papers (papers on which an effective subsequent preference is not shown). If the surplus is equal to or greater than the number of transferable votes, each remaining candidate will receive all the votes from the appropriate parcel of transferable papers. For example, in the fictitious three-seat LEA mentioned above, candidate A has been elected with a total of 2,891 votes. Her surplus is therefore 748 votes (2,891 minus 2,143) and these votes are distributed according to the next available preference on the ballot papers.

Where the surplus is less than the number of transferable papers each remaining candidate will receive from the appropriate parcel of transferable papers a number of votes calculated as follows: surplus multiplied by the number of papers in parcel divided by the total number of transferable papers. If the surplus arises out of transferred papers, only the papers in the parcel last transferred to that candidate are examined and this parcel is then treated in the same way as a surplus consisting of first preference votes. An explanation for this is provided by way of an example on the website of the Department of the Environment, Heritage and Local Government, as follows: If candidate A was 6 votes short of the quota and then got 10 votes in a particular count, she would have a surplus of 4 votes. The 10 votes that got her elected are examined and 8 are found to be transferable, viz. 6 to candidate C and 2 to candidate D. The ratio of the surplus of 4 votes to the 8 transferable papers in A's last parcel of votes is 0.5. This ratio is applied to the sub-parcels of next preferences for candidates C and D. Thus, the votes transferred in the distribution of A's surplus of 4 votes are the top 3 votes in the sub-parcel of next preferences for candidate C, together with the top vote in the sub-parcel of next preferences for candidate D.

If two or more candidates exceed the quota, the larger surplus is distributed first. In the event that no candidate has a surplus or the surplus is insufficient to elect one of the remaining candidates or materially affect the progress of the count, the lowest of the remaining candidates is eliminated and her or his papers are transferred to remaining candidates according to the next available preference. If a ballot paper is to be transferred and the second preference shown on it is for a candidate already elected or eliminated, the vote passes to the third choice and so on. Counting continues until all the seats have been filled. If the number of seats left to be filled is equal to the number of candidates still in the running, those remaining candidates are declared elected without having reached the quota. Even the most experienced election watchers can find the PR-STV system complex. The following example from the 2004 local elections illustrates how the system operates.

The example comes from the Dingle LEA, which elects three members to Kerry County Council. The total electorate for the Dingle LEA in 2004 was 11,918. From this electorate, 8,238 valid ballots were cast, representing a turnout of 69 per cent. The quota was accordingly calculated as 2,060.

$$8,238 / (3+1) +1 = 2,060$$

Seven candidates contested the election and received the following first preference votes:

DINGLE LEA, FIRST COUNT, 2004 (QUOTA OF 2,060)

Candidate	Affiliation	1st Preferences
Michael O'Shea	Fianna Fáil	1,898
Breandán MacGearailt	Fianna Fáil	1,613
Seamus Fitzgerald	Fine Gael	1,565
Brigid O'Connor	Independent	1,196
Brendan Griffin	Fine Gael	1,044
Owen O'Shea	Labour Party	577
Pat O'Shea	Sinn Féin	345

No candidate was elected as a result of the first preferences because the quota of 2,060 was not reached. As the lowest-ranking candidates, Pat O'Shea and Owen O'Shea were eliminated and their second preferences were distributed. The Labour Party and Sinn Féin candidates received a combined total of 922 votes of which 111 were non-transferable (i.e. no second preference was indicated). Therefore, 811 votes were divided out amongst the remaining five candidates.

DINGLE LEA, SECOND COUNT, 2004 (QUOTA OF 2,060)

Candidate	Affiliation	1st Preferences + Transfers
Michael O'Shea	Fianna Fáil	1,898 + 189 = 2,087 [Elected]
Breandán MacGearailt	Fianna Fáil	1,613 + 82 = 1,695
Seamus Fitzgerald	Fine Gael	1,565 + 108 = 1,673
Brigid O'Connor	Independent	1,196 + 237 = 1,433
Brendan Griffin	Fine Gael	1,044 + 195 = 1,239
Owen O'Shea	Labour Party	Eliminated
Pat O'Shea	Sinn Féin	Eliminated

At this stage, with the 189 transfer votes received, Fianna Fáil's Michael O'Shea, was deemed elected as his total of votes exceeded the quota. Brendan Griffin of Fine Gael was then eliminated and his 1,239 were distributed, of which 940 were transferable.

DINGLE LEA, THIRD COUNT, 2004 (QUOTA OF 2,060)

Candidate	Affiliation	1st Preferences + Transfers
Michael O'Shea	Fianna Fáil	1,898 + 189 = 2,087 [Elected]
Seamus Fitzgerald	Fine Gael	1,673 + 490 = 2,163 [Elected]
Breandán MacGearailt	Fianna Fáil	1,695 + 139 = 1,834
Brigid O'Connor	Independent	1,433 + 311 = 1,744
Brendan Griffin	Fine Gael	Eliminated
Owen O'Shea	Labour Party	Eliminated
Pat O'Shea	Sinn Féin	Eliminated

Boosted by the transfers of his party colleague, Fine Gael's Seamus Fitzgerald was now deemed elected, having exceeded the quota. With three candidates eliminated and two elected, the final seat now became a straight fight between Breandán MacGearailt and Brigid O'Connor. Fitzgerald's surplus of 103 votes (the amount in excess of the quota) was then distributed between MacGearailt and O'Connor.

DINGLE LEA, FOURTH COUNT, 2004 (QUOTA OF 2,060)

Candidate	Affiliation	1st Preferences + Transfers
Michael O'Shea	Fianna Fáil	1,898 + 189 = 2,087 [Elected]
Seamus Fitzgerald	Fine Gael	1,673 + 490 = 2,163 [Elected]
Breandán MacGearailt	Fianna Fáil	1,834 + 38 = 1,872 [Elected]
Brigid O'Connor	Independent	1,744 + 65 = 1,809
Brendan Griffin	Fine Gael	Eliminated
Owen O'Shea	Labour Party	Eliminated
Pat O'Shea	Sinn Féin	Eliminated

The count was now complete and, even though he had not achieved the quota, Breandán MacGearailt claimed the final seat from the Dingle LEA.

Recounts and challenges

A returning officer may recount all or any of the papers at any stage of a count. A candidate or the election agent of a candidate is entitled to ask for a recount of the papers dealt with at a particular count or to ask for one complete recount of all the parcels of ballot papers. When recounting, the order of the papers must not be disturbed. When a significant error is discovered, the papers must be counted afresh from the point at which the error occurred.

When the count is completed, the returning officer declares and gives public notice of the results of the election and returns the names of the elected members to the local authority concerned. If a candidate has been elected as a member in more than one electoral area, they must, within three days of the public notice of the results, declare in writing which area they wish to represent.

Any person aged eighteen or over may question the outcome of a local election by way of petition in the Circuit Court within twenty-eight days of the declaration of the results. The election may be questioned on grounds of want of qualification, obstruction of or interference with or other hindrance to the conduct of the election, or mistake or other irregularity. The Circuit Court, at the trial of an election petition, must determine the correct result of the election and, for this purpose, may order the votes to be recounted. The Court may declare the whole or part of the election in the constituency void and, in that event, a fresh election will be held to fill the vacant seats.

Casual vacancies arising in the membership of elected local authorities – typically by death, resignation or disquali - fication – are filled by co-option by the authority concerned. The co-opted member holds the seat until the next election under the same conditions as elected councillors. Co-option was introduced by the act of 1898 but was updated by the 2001 legislation, which provides that the co-optee must be a member of the same party as the person causing the vacancy. In the case of a non-party councillor, the vacancy is filled in accordance with the local authority's standing orders. Co-option can be criticised on the grounds that it fosters nepotism (see chapter 5 for more details) and is not truly democratic but the alternative of holding local bye-elections is not always feasible.

Election spending

The Local Elections (Disclosure of Donations and Expenditure) Act 1999, as amended by the Electoral (Amendment) Act 2001, provides for an expenditure and donation disclosure regime at local elections. The donation limit for disclosure purposes is €634.87. If a candidate receives a donation for a political activity in any calendar year which is greater than €126.97, he or she must open and maintain a bank account in a financial institution of the state. The maximum limit for a political donation from any one source in a year is €2,539.48 while foreign and anonymous donations cannot go above €126.97.

Until 2009 there were no limits on spending at local elections. A Fine Gael candidate for the Dún Laoghaire LEA, Eugene Regan, spent €45,000 on his campaign in 2004.[9] Regan secured 1,957 first preference votes (effectively €23 per vote) and was elected on the seventh count to Dún Laoghaire–Rathdown County Council.

The 2007 programme for government committed to the introduction of expenditure limits on electoral spending for local elections, analogous to that which applies at Dáil elections. In February 2009 Minister Gormley announced that all candidates standing in local elections will be subject to limits on election expenditure. The thirty-four local authorities at county and city level have a sliding scale with four different spending limits depending on population size. The four limits are €15,000, €13,000, €11,500 and €9,750. For borough and town council elections, a standard limit of €7,500 applies. Candidates nominated by a political party will be deemed to allocate automatically 10 per cent of their limit for use by the party's national agent. The position is as follows:

- For a county/city council electoral area with a population of 32,501 or over, the spending limit is €15,000. The effective limit for the candidate is €13,500 after the 10 per cent (€1,500) is allocated to the political party.
- For a county/city council electoral area with a population between 22,501 and 32,500, the spending limit is €13,000. The effective limit for the candidate is €11,700 after the 10 per cent (€1,300) is allocated to the political party.
- For a county/city council electoral area with a population between 12,001 and 22,500, the spending limit is €11,500. The effective limit for the candidate is €10,350 after the 10 per cent (€1,150) is allocated to the political party.
- For a county/city council electoral area with a population less than 12,000, the spending limit is €9,750. The effective limit for the candidate is €8,775 after the 10 per cent (€975) is allocated to the political party.
- For all borough and town councils, the spending limit is €7,500. The effective limit for the candidate is €6,750 after the 10 per cent (€750) is allocated to the political party.

Minister Gormley stated that the spending limits would create a level playing field for candidates and he promised that legislation would be in place in time for the 2009 elections. Candidates will continue to submit spending returns to their local authority but must now comply with the new limits.

Election posters and signs

Irish law forbids the putting up of posters or signs on poles or other structures in public places unless one has obtained the written permission of the owner in advance. There are no rules in place regarding how far in advance of a local election that posters and signs can be erected. However, local authorities have the power to introduce bye-laws if they so choose to specify when promotional material can be erected. Local authorities also have the power to remove these items should they disintegrate or cause a litter nuisance. Following an election, a party/candidate must remove posters within a seven-day period. After that date, an on-the-spot fine of €125 is issued by the local authority in respect of each remaining poster. The local authority will remove the poster as the fine is issued. If a party/candidate has been issued with a fine and refuses to pay, they can be prosecuted in the District Court by the local authority to enforce payment. The maximum penalty in the District Court following conviction for non-payment of the fine is €1,900. In July 2008, the Minister for the Environment, Heritage and Local Government launched a public consultation process on the subject of election and referendum posters. At the time of going to press, it was expected that legislation amending the litter pollution acts and restricting the locations in which posters can be displayed would be introduced during 2009.

Conclusion

The present local electoral arrangements in Ireland are straightforward and are based on the premise that you do not have to be an Irish citizen to vote in or contest an election. There are at present over 3 million local government electors in Ireland. Having outlined the rules and procedures governing local elections, in the next chapter we present some of the interesting facts, figures and stories from the twenty-two county and city councils election held during the period from 1899 to 2004.

4

Local Elections, 1899–2004

Vote for my party in particular ME
If I get your vote I will make this decree –
Water rates will dry up and you won't need much pull
To get on the housing list extended – not full
There'll be jobs for the boys and jobs for the girlies
For the GAA players no tax on the hurleys
What will pay for these blessings both urban and rural?
I'll give up my junkets and my pensions – PLURAL

The above poem was composed by Margery Brady as a campaign ditty for an election competition in *The Irish Times* (24 June 1985). It captures much of what the local election in Ireland is all about, which is described in more detail in this chapter, dating back to the first elections held in 1899. It is beyond the scope of this book to analyse each of the twenty-two county council elections in depth; rather it is our aim to give a flavour of the local election process by describing some of the colour, excitement and controversy of local contests down through the years. Local elections have not always been held on the one day and sometimes have been stretched over significant periods of time. A notable example is the 1934 elections, which were spread over June, July and November. With this caveat in mind, table 4.1 below details the dates of local county and borough elections held since the act of 1898.

TABLE **4.1** DATES OF COUNTY COUNCIL ELECTIONS, **1899–2009**

1.	1899: 6 April	13.	1950: 20 September
2.	1902: 28 May	14.	1955: 23 June–1 July
3.	1905: 2 June	15.	1960: 23 June–1 July
4.	1908: 1 June	16.	1967: 28 June
5.	1911: 31 May	17.	1974: 18 June
6.	1914: 4 June	18.	1979: 7 June
7.	1920: 2 June	19.	1985: 20 June
8.	1925: 18–23 June	20.	1991: 27 June
9.	1928: 26 June	21.	1999: 11 June
10.	1934: June, July and November	22.	2004: 11 June
11.	1942: 19 August	23.	2009: 5 June
12.	1945: 14 June		

Source: Department of the Environment, Heritage and Local Government; various local and national newspapers.

In most cases, sub-county (e.g. town council) elections are held on the same day as county and city elections but this is not always the case. In 1991, for example, elections took place for counties and cities only and the sub-county elections did not happen until the summer of 1994. Local elections are quite often held in conjunction with other votes. The 1945 local election coincided with Ireland's first contested presidential election, won by Seán T. O'Kelly. In 1979, the local elections were run on the same day as the first direct elections to the European Parliament. At the local elections of 1999 and 2004, the electorate was also asked to vote on national referenda (as well as European Parliament elections). The referendum in 1999, as previously mentioned, related to constitutional recognition of local government, membership of the International Criminal Court, abolishment of the death penalty and, in 2004, national citizenship.

It was only in 1974 that the Department of the Environment began to produce details of the local election results. Obtaining local election data for the years prior to 1974 is extremely difficult as their availability is dependent on the willingness of newspapers to publish such results. While chapter 7 provides more detail on turnout, it has been clear for some time that the highest participation levels come from rural areas. Low participation in the cities, especially Dublin, is a problem as illustrated by the following tables, which show the lowest and highest LEA turnouts in 2004.

TABLE 4.2 LOWEST TEN LOCAL ELECTORAL AREAS BY TURNOUT, 2004

Local Electoral Area	Local Authority	Turnout (%)
North Inner City	Dublin City Council	42.3
South West Inner City	Dublin City Council	43.6
South East Inner City	Dublin City Council	44.8
Rathmines	Dublin City Council	45.8
Tallaght South	South Dublin County Council	45.9
Trim	Meath County Council	47.1
Celbridge	Kildare County Council	47.7
Clondalkin	South Dublin County Council	47.7
Ballyfermot	Dublin City Council	49.2
Carlow Town No. 1	Carlow County Council	49.5

Source: Adrian Kavanagh (2004), 'The 2004 Local Elections in the Republic of Ireland', *Irish Political Studies*, 19 (2), p. 68.

TABLE 4.3 HIGHEST TEN LOCAL ELECTORAL AREAS BY TURNOUT, **2004**

Local Electoral Area	Local Authority	Turnout (%)
Ballinamore	Leitrim County Council	76.3
Dromahaire	Leitrim County Council	75.8
Mountmellick	Laois County Council	75.6
Tobercurry	Sligo County Council	75.1
Ballinrobe	Mayo County Council	73.2
Carrickmacross	Monaghan County Council	73.2
Drumlish	Longford County Council	72.0
Ballymote	Sligo County Council	71.6
Ballymahon	Longford County Council	71.6
Killarney	Kerry County Council	71.5

Source: Adrian Kavanagh (2004), 'The 2004 Local Elections in the Republic of Ireland', *Irish Political Studies*, 19 (2), p. 68.

Based on the above figures, it is no surprise that Dublin city was bottom of the class in terms of turnout at the 2004 elections with an average of 52 per cent while Leitrim was at the top with 73 per cent. As poor as the Dublin figures are, it is worth reflecting that they represent a major improvement from the 1999 local elections. Ballyfermot had a turnout of 49 per cent in 2004 but was as low as 29 per cent five years previously.

Past Local Elections

The 1899 local elections were truly historic and were a revolution in Irish local government. Though reaction to the new system varied across the country, for the most part the elections generated excitement and, in some cases, violence. At an election meeting in Skibbereen, County Cork, a farmer died after an onlooker struck him with a stone. In Killarney, a pre-election rally held by Lord Castlerose and his nationalist competitor descended to fisticuffs, described as follows:[1]

> Mr Crean, who by this time looked like a miller immersed in a vat of egg flip and Mr Moriarty who was little better off and his supporters made an essay to mount a donkey cart to address the crowd, but a shower of eggs and stones fell among them and then the cordon of police was broken through and blows with large sticks and stone-laden fists were freely exchanged.

Polling day, 6 April, was very busy with over 4,000 district elections taking place. Poor weather conditions caused problems and, undoubtedly, affected turnout. No national turnout figures were compiled but it was reported that in the Carrick-on-Suir division of South Tipperary more than 75 per cent of electors cast a vote. According to the Local Government Board the day passed off without problems, the tragic exception being the drowning of two fishermen returning to the mainland following canvassing on Aran Island.[2] Women and illiterate voters received a lot of coverage in the local media. In the Blarney division for the Cork County Council elections, it was reported that by 4 p.m. thirty-six out of a possible forty-seven women had voted. Of the first seventy-nine people who went to cast a vote for the Cork County Council elections in the Kilcullen division, it was noted that only nine could read and write.[3]

The election results were dramatic. Prior to 1899, unionists held 704 Grand Jury seats, compared to 47 for nationalists. After the elections, the balance of power shifted completely with nationalists taking 774 of the new council seats. Unionists won 265 seats, the majority of which were in Ulster. A newspaper article reported: '[…] the results were everywhere received with good humour and satisfaction. The successful candidates did not boast their victory nor did the defeated see any reason for undue depressions or disappointment'.[4] This is only partly true as a certain amount of celebratory boasting took place in Dungarvan, Waterford, where bonfires burned on the hills around the town. The local newspaper declared that the bonfires marked a people rejoicing because, for the first time in the country's chequered history, the voice of the people had been allowed to assert itself and representatives of the crown colony were now being replaced by representatives chosen by the people.[5] Other areas of the country, including Tralee, Kerry, marked the local election results with marching bands and torchlight processions. The change in local government personnel in 1899 is reflected by the composition of the new 35-member Galway County Council, which included 18 tenant farmers, a Catholic unionist barrister and writer, 3 solicitors, a college professor and medical doctor, 3 merchants, an auctioneer and 1 landlord.

Over the next fifteen years, five sets of local government elections were held on a triennial basis. While they failed to create the same excitement as the inaugural elections in 1899 they constituted a democratisation of the system (which later evolved into politicisation).[6] Local government during this period very much reflected national politics. Consequently, the Nationalist Party was dominant at both national and local levels.

The local elections of 1920 warrant a special mention as they were a pivotal event during the transitional years from the Easter Rising in 1916, through the War of Independence, the emergence of the Free State in 1922 and the subsequent civil war. Sinn Féin, reconstituted as a republican party in 1917 with the stated aim of establishing an all-Ireland republic, enjoyed a spectacular success in the general election of 1918 and fought the local elections two years later in a position of strength. The local elections in 1920 gained extra significance because no local elections had been held for six years and the revolutionary backdrop provided an added national political dimension. Sinn Féin promised to clean up local government as the Nationalist Party struggled to detach itself from allegations of corruption, patronage and financial mismanagement. Above all else, the 1920 local elections were used as a platform to defy English political control. *The Irish Times* of 8 June 1920 reported that, in Dublin, Sinn Féin brought voters to the polling stations in cars and other vehicles flying the tricolour. The polls confirmed Sinn Féin's dominance in 28 out of 33 county councils and 172 out of 206 boroughs and urban districts. Philip Monahan – later Ireland's first local authority manager – topped the poll in Drogheda Borough Corporation and, during a victorious torchlit procession through the town, gave a speech in which he asserted that Sinn Féin had delivered a message of defiance to the world that Irish people were unalterably determined to be free from England.[7] In Cork, the Lord Mayor, William F. O'Connor, was elected in three separate constituencies within the city corporation. Thus the opportunity was afforded to two of his Sinn Féin colleagues to take their places on the corporation and this swelled the party's representation to thirty-two of the fifty-six seats. During 1920, local government in Cork – and especially the office of Lord Mayor – gained national and international coverage. First, Tomás MacCurtain, the Sinn Féin mayor, was killed by British forces on 20 March in his Blackpool home in Cork city. Secondly, MacCurtain's successor, Terence McSwiney, was arrested on charges of possession of a British cypher code machine and died on hunger strike in Brixton Prison on 25 October. When arrested, McSwiney had refused to part with his mayoral chain of office; his defiance enhanced the position of Lord Mayor and local government in Cork. Another interesting footnote to the 1920 local elections is that the system of proportional representation was used nationally for the first time following legislation enacted in 1919.

The notable feature of the 1925 local elections is that there were no contests in Kerry, Leitrim and Offaly County Councils and the Cork and Dublin Corporations as the councils had been dissolved and replaced by commissioners (see chapter 2). In 1925, the government – in the aftermath of the civil war – was determined to make local government as technocratic and de-politicised as possible. Perhaps this is reflected in the low turnout that year with *The Irish Times* complaining about the apparent apathy of ratepayers. The local elections of 1928 were also low key but it is interesting that they 'were largely free of the dominance of national parties'[8] and we began to see the emergence of candidates mobilised on single issues and influenced by local concerns as opposed to national ones.

By the 1934 elections, the picture had changed due to the emergence of the Fianna Fáil party which won general elections in 1932 and 1933. Fianna Fáil took control in the majority of local authorities in 1934 and a new period began – which some would say lasts to the present day – whereby 'local elections once again began to shadow national elections, though showing some interesting and rather characteristic deviations from the pattern of national politics'.[9] Some of these deviations were apparent in the next elections held in 1942. In the run-up to the elections, *The Irish Times* urged voters to disregard politics and vote for the people best suited to public administration. The Irish electorate took this advice on board with the election of a significant number of Independent candidates. Independents took 24 per cent of the votes (172 seats), making them the second-largest grouping after Fianna Fáil. Again, however, apathy was a problem and turnout was at a lowly 40 per cent in Dublin. The 1945 local elections received little media attention as the newspapers were dominated by the presidential election held on the same day. One concerned elector did, however, write a letter to *The Irish Times* on 18 June in which he stated that, while proportional representation had many advantages, elections were largely decided by the order of names as printed on ballot papers. As an example to illustrate his point, the elector showed that in the Dublin Corporation election, four of the nine areas elected the candidate whose name appeared first on the ballot paper. Of thirty-two candidates with the initial B or C, twenty-two won seats. Alphabetical order was not an issue in the 1950 election for Kinsale Urban District Council as the main parties reached a gentleman's agreement on nomination day not to contest the election, citing the interests of economy of expenditure. The main controversy in 1950 appears to have come after the elections, with confusion as to who was responsible for removing posters.

By 1955, local elections had moved to a five-year cycle, and the high levels of domestic rates dominated the campaign. The Ratepayers' Association emerged as a strong group and made a big impact in Dublin city. In the corporation elections, Fianna Fáil and Fine Gael each lost four seats and the Ratepayers claimed six of them. In Donegal, the election of the Independent Samuel Baxter from the Letterkenny electoral area was noteworthy as the candidate was in his eightieth year. The build-up to the 1960 local elections was dominated by predictions of low turnout due to a spell of fine weather, the Canada Cup golf tournament (now called the World Cup, it took place in Portmarnock in 1960 and was won by the American duo Arnold Palmer and Sam Snead) and what *The Irish Times* (23 June) described as 'the obvious apathy'. While interest may have been lacking amongst the electorate, a staggering 149 candidates contested the 45 seats on Dublin Corporation. The turnout predictions proved correct and Minister for Local Government, Neil Blaney TD, subsequently challenged members of the Dáil to come up with ideas as to how to get more people to vote. In response to the suggestion that elections might be held on Sundays, Minister Blaney argued that there would be objections on religious grounds.

There was a seven-year gap before the next local elections in the summer of 1967. A much bigger poll than in 1960 was attributed to a concerted offensive from the opposition parties, Fine Gael and Labour. It was also felt that there was a strong protest vote, which had continued on from the previous year's presidential election when Éamon de Valera had narrowly defeated Tom O'Higgins. A dispute involving the National Farmers' Association (now the Irish Farmers' Association) helped to boost the polls in the west, southeast and midlands. The highest vote in the country was recorded in Ballybay, County Monaghan, at 90 per cent. The national averages of 71 per cent at county and city level and 67 per cent across all the local authorities have not been reached in the intervening forty-two years. Broadly reflecting the national political picture, the three main parties, Fianna Fáil, Fine Gael and Labour, dominated proceedings, leading the political correspondent of *The Irish Times* (1 July) to predict that, apart from in Cork and Dublin, Independent candidates would have no future in the Irish electoral scene.

Polling was down 5 per cent in 1974 with a bus strike and a World Cup game (this time of the football variety) between Scotland and Brazil dealing a body blow to turnout in Dublin, according to the local government correspondent of *The Irish Times*. He explained that the situation was better in the provinces because, as GAA strongholds, there would be 'absolutely no interest in the World Cup' (19 June). A key issue on the campaign trail in 1974 was whether candidates should declare any interest they might have in building or property businesses. Niall Andrews of Fianna Fáil criticised those in property and building who stood for election, many of whom, he said, found their way onto local council planning committees and used their positions to launch careers in land speculation. From a political perspective, the coalition parties retained control of a majority of local authorities in the state although Fianna Fáil won control of Cork Corporation for the first time. After the election, the Minister for Local Government, James Tully, announced that he was considering the introduction of legislation to deal with situations where county councillors were interested in land or land transactions where value could be added by planning decisions.

Candidates and canvassers alike claimed that the 1979 local elections were very difficult for them. There were a variety of reasons for this. The local contests were greatly overshadowed by the European Parliament elections and the combination of elections caused confusion amongst the electorate. Due to a postal strike, candidates were unable to distribute campaign literature as they would have wished. In addition, petrol shortages curtailed canvassing efforts. Another element in 1979 was the growing feeling that local government was irrelevant and toothless, a viewpoint strengthened by the abolition of domestic rates through legislation in 1978. Local authorities having responsibility but no power was a phrase seen a lot in newspapers during the build-up to election day. The emergence of female candidates was the big story of the 1979 local elections. In 1967, 118 women stood for local election, a figure which rose to 169 in 1974. Fine Gael alone ran almost 160 women in 1979 and the total across the country was approximately 300. In the aftermath of the elections, Fine Gael leader, Garret FitzGerald, stated, 'Anyone who tries to deny that there is a women's vote after this is ignoring reality'.[10] For the second successive local elections, Fianna Fáil lost ground with a swing towards Fine Gael.

The all-too-familiar combination of apathy and bad weather affected polling at the 1985 local elections with a 60 per cent national turnout. Campaigning had been lacklustre with little public interest in proceedings and no major issues emerging. The coalition government parties of Fine Gael and Labour suffered badly at the polls with Fianna Fáil, unsurprisingly, regaining the ground it had lost over the previous two elections. The Taoiseach of the time, Garret FitzGerald, declared that local democracy (as opposed to the government) was the real loser because so few people turned out to vote. In Cork, a rank outsider, the Independent candidate Bernard 'Bernie' Murphy, was elected to the Corporation. Murphy, who could not read or write, was well known in the city as a sandwich-board advertising man and his election represented a major betting coup, with local bookmakers paying out more than £20,000 as many people had placed large sums of money on the 50–1 outsider. Murphy spent six colourful years on Cork Corporation and he gained publicity in 1986 when he went on an official visit to San Francisco, Cork's twin city, in search of a new set of false teeth. Bernie Murphy's famous 1985 election poster is now a valuable collector's item. The poster showed Murphy's face superimposed on a pint of stout with the slogan, 'Murphy – The People's Champion – Here's Up Them All.' An interesting situation arose in Leitrim where Pat Gallagher, a local authority rate collector in Donegal, won a seat on the county council. Under the terms of the 1955 Local Government Act, Gallagher was required to either forfeit his council seat or resign from his local authority job; he chose the former.

A poll by the Market Research Bureau of Ireland (MRBI) before the 1991 elections showed that local issues, such as roads, water supplies, refuse collections and local charges, were the main concern among voters. In answer to the question 'In your opinion, are local elections only about local issues or are they about how parties are performing on national issues?', of those surveyed, 47 per cent went for local issues only, 30 per cent opted for national issues, with 19 per cent indicating that local and national considerations were of equal importance (4 per cent expressed no opinion). Turnout slipped a further 4 per cent from 1985 and the elections brought no great comfort to the larger political parties. The Progressive Democrats and the Green Party enjoyed limited success and widened the spread of representation, which the proportional representation system was designed to achieve. Female candidates generally did not fare as well as had been expected with the 'Mary Robinson effect' not significant. Just as Garret FitzGerald had downplayed the local election results in 1985, so too did Taoiseach Charles J. Haughey in 1991, stating, 'The local elections were very largely focused on local issues and even single issues such as hospitals and roads in certain areas, and so they don't have, as far as I am concerned, any particular implications for national politics'.[11] One defeated local candidate, Emmett M. J. McElhatton, explained in verse (*The Irish Times*, 8 July 1991) how the election had gone for him:

How many babies have I kissed?
Not many meetings have I missed.
I've endured so many boring talks,
My feet still ache from sponsored walks.
Countless funerals, endless graves,
Walking all those Churches' naves.
Every local cause I've backed,
Enthusiasm I've never lacked.
It seems now it was all in vain,
Defeat inflicts such bitter pain.

Voters had to wait eight years for their next opportunity to participate in the local electoral process. The 1999 local elections marked the centenary of the first historic elections in 1899. The campaign failed to explode into life, partly because there was no universal local government issue. Turnout fell to its lowest ever recorded level with polling at an average of 51 per cent nationally. The number of candidates offering themselves for election fell by 135. A significant feature of the 1999 elections is that 40 per cent of the outgoing 883 councillors were not returned. One reason for this relatively high figure is that the government introduced a gratuity scheme to reward veteran councillors and encourage some of them to leave and pave the way for new members to enter the system. The gratuity scheme (referred to within local authorities as the 'scrappage scheme') offered £750 per year for the first twenty years of service at county level and £500 per year for a further twenty. The election results confirmed the electorate's preference for the traditional parties; Fianna Fáil (up twenty-five seats) and Fine Gael (up seven seats) made modest gains at the expense of the Labour

Party and the Progressive Democrats. Sinn Féin enjoyed a breakthrough success with its presence in local councils increasing from seven seats to twenty-one. Female candidates took 15 per cent of the seats, a 3 per cent improvement from 1991. The local elections of 1999 also saw the continuation, and strengthening, of family dynasties. The Taoiseach Bertie Ahern saw his two brothers, Maurice and Noel, elected to Dublin Corporation; they were joined by Seán Haughey (son of former Taoiseach, Charles J. Haughey), and Chris Andrews (son of Niall Andrews MEP). Chris' cousin, Barry, son of the Minister for Foreign Affairs, David Andrews, was elected to Dún Laoghaire Corporation. John Hanafin, sister of Mary Hanafin, was elected to Tipperary County Council and the brothers of three cabinet ministers, Micheál Martin, John O'Donoghue and Brian Cowen, were elected. Husband and wife duo, Seán Ardagh (Dublin Corporation) and Marie Ardagh (Dublin South County Council) were both successful. The sons of Ministers of State Joe Jacob, Danny Wallace and Ned O'Keefe all won council seats, as did the son of Fianna Fáil Parliamentary Party chairman Rory O'Hanlon. Fine Gael, too, saw family members of senior figures elected. Fionnuala Dukes, wife of former leader Alan Dukes, was elected in Kildare. In Dún Laoghaire–Rathdown, Louise Cosgrave, granddaughter of the former Taoiseach William T. Cosgrave, was elected.[12] Despite the simultaneous holding of a constitutional referendum and European Parliament elections, the 1999 local elections failed to excite the public and the continuing downward trend in turnout suggested that 'for the branch of our democracy occupied by local government there was a growing degree of public indifference'.[13]

The local elections in 2004 saw a welcome increase in turnout to a 59 per cent national average. There was strong coverage by local and national radio and media and 'it seemed as if every telephone pole in city and county was festooned with images of carefully coiffured candidates'.[14] Polling booths were open for fourteen hours from 7 a.m. to 9 p.m. and the electorate responded with the highest participation since 1985. Since the previous elections in 1999 there had been some changes to the local government landscape. The referendum passed in 1999 inserted a specific local government recognition in the constitution and guaranteed the holding of local elections every five years; a representational payment, a pension scheme and increased expense allowances were introduced for councillors and the Local Government Act, 2003, ended the dual mandate. As in previous local elections, no single issue either dominated the campaign or unified the electorate but planning concerns were prominent, especially the politically sensitive question of one-off rural housing. The dual mandate ban led to ninety-nine Oireachtas members who were councillors giving up their council seats before the election. Most did so in 2003 with the aid of a generous financial inducement, and family members were generally co-opted in their places (see chapter 5 for more details).

Politically, the 2004 local elections were a disaster for Fianna Fáil. The party suffered its worst election results in eighty years, and it lost 9 per cent of its seats (eighty seats in total). A notable Fianna Fáil casualty was in Clare where it ceded control of the county council for the first time in seventy years. With the ominous exception of the Progressive

Democrats, all the other political parties shared in the spoils of Fianna Fáil's dramatic loss. While Taoiseach Bertie Ahern acknowledged that Sinn Féin won the elections (it increased its number of seats from twenty-one to fifty-four), this intentionally downplayed Fine Gael's performance. Fine Gael benefited more from the Fianna Fáil collapse than anyone else; the party came within nine seats of Fianna Fáil, the closest gap in modern local electoral history. The breakdown of the 883 seats on Ireland's thirty-four county and city councils after the 2004 elections was as follows:

TABLE **4.4** REPRESENTATION OF PARTIES ON CITY AND COUNCIL
COUNCILS, 2004

Party	Number of Seats
Fianna Fáil	302
Fine Gael	293
Labour Party	101
Non-Party (Independents)	89
Sinn Féin	54
Progressive Democrats	19
Green Party	18
Other Parties*	7
Total	883

* The category 'Other Parties' comprises the Socialist Party, the Workers' Party and the South Kerry Independent Alliance.

Predictably, Fianna Fáil lost control of many local authorities in 2004 and Fine Gael held the most mayoral posts. Time will tell 'whether these elections ultimately prove to be particularly ground-breaking and a historic signpost or else prove to be a temporary aberration to the trends of continued

Fianna Fáil hegemony and turnout decline'.[15] Female representation increased to 17 per cent in 2004 but women still find it difficult to make a major breakthrough into the Irish local government system. Reflecting the change in Ireland's demographic structure, two black candidates won town council seats in 2004. Dr Taiwo Matthew was elected in Ennis and Rotimi Adebari in Portlaoise; Adebari has since gone on to become Ireland's first black mayor. Since all Irish residents regardless of nationality can both run and vote at local elections, it is perhaps surprising that the new wave of immigration has not had a greater impact at local government level. This is something that may change at future elections.

Conclusion

Local elections in Ireland have had a chequered history, punctuated by regular postponements. In spite of this, since the first elections 110 years ago, there have been twenty-two sets of local elections, which means that, on average, elections have taken place every five years. This is one trend that should continue due to constitutional recognition and electoral legislation. Other trends are more difficult to analyse. As we will see in chapter 7, participation in the electoral process has varied significantly over the years; the turnout in 2004 was the highest in twenty years and bucked the steady downward trend of previous contests. The early local elections were highly politicised but there then followed a period where there was an attempt to de-politicise local government. Recent elections have again tended to be political and regarded as a miniature general election. The analysis of local elections is often reduced to a commentary about what the results would mean if they had occurred in a general election. One interesting feature of local elections is the kind of people who offer themselves before the electorate and this facet of Irish local elections is discussed in chapter 5. As suggested by the verse below – again taken from the newspaper competition referred to at the beginning of the chapter – the ideal local election candidate should have, amongst other attributes, an aptitude for balancing facts and figures as well as being honest, clean-living and intelligent.

> May I introduce you, madam,
> To my good friend here – Sinclair
> He is running for election
> And he really has a flair
> For balancing facts and figures
> For understanding tax
> As for water-rates and housing loans
> He truly knows his facts.
> He is honest, clean, good-living
> Doesn't drink or smoke
> Never makes false promises
> Or cracks a nasty joke.
> He's quick-witted, intelligent
> – No candidate's 'astuter' –
> Please, madam, give your no. 1
> To Sinclair – the computer!
> (Gerry Moran, *The Irish Times,* 24 June 1985)

Whether the average candidate drinks and smokes or has a flair for balancing figures is discussed in the next chapter.

5

Local Election Candidates

The nature and tone of local elections is in large part set by those contesting them. However, while we know a reasonable amount about the type of candidate who contests national elections, there are far less data available on local election candidates. We know, for example, that the average candidate at a general election is more likely to be older, better-educated, wealthier, middle-class and of the male sex than the average voter.[1] Do local election candidates exhibit the same traits, or does the local arena have an institutional effect and produce a different type of candidate? Using data from a survey of candidates from the 2004 local elections, this chapter provides some answers to these questions. Details are provided on the background of local election candidates and their motivations for running. This data is then used in the conclusion to construct a typology of the individuals who run for local office in Ireland.

Why run for political office?

To discover the motives of local election candidates, those running for city and council elections in 2004 were sent a mail survey (see Appendix 2 for more details). It is interesting to understand why these particular individuals (a few thousand in the case of local elections), from a potential several million, choose to run for political office. When the vast majority do not even consider throwing their hat into the ring, why does a relative handful go against the grain? Is there something in their individual psyche compelling them to sample political life? Perhaps they are simply following in a family tradition; or maybe they are power-hungry individuals who see local government as simply the first rung on the ladder to the Taoiseach's office? Some may even leave the final decision to chance. Before handing in his nomination papers for the Dáil election of 1948, first-time candidate (and future Taoiseach) Jack Lynch had some doubts about a foray into politics; he could not come to a fixed decision, so he chose to determine his fate on the toss of a coin.[2]

Of course, it is not the case that the population is divided into two camps: those who run for office and those who do not. Amongst the general public, there are many potential candidates interested in political activism, yet for a variety of reasons only a few decide to run. This area of research is known as 'candidate emergence', which is a fusion of several sub-fields of political science, most notably political participation and political recruitment. The choice of words is deliberate, as it suggests that potential candidates exist everywhere, but that they emerge only in certain situations and contexts.[3] There has been only limited research conducted in this area, which is strange because there is so much focus on why voters choose one of the few candidates available, yet very little study of why the candidates are whittled down to these few in the first place.[4] The aim of this chapter is to shed some light on this area, in particular by focusing on local candidates' incentives for running and their sociological background. We are interested in observing whether candidates in Ireland are any different from those in other societies, or whether the nature of politics will always attract a particular type of individual, regardless of the context.

Analysing candidates' incentives

To understand why local election candidates run, the direct route of asking them is the first obvious method. However, rather than giving an open, honest answer, some candidates may be more inclined to state a reason that portrays them in a favourable light. In addition, open-ended questions often result in idiosyncratic responses that can be difficult to categorise, and where candidates state a number of factors (as is often the case), it is impossible to know the individual contribution of each factor. To overcome this problem, candidates were given a number of possible reasons for running, and asked to rank how important each of these was on a scale of 1 to 10 in motivating their decision to run for office (where 1 was 'not at all important', and 10 'extremely important'). They were also given the opportunity to add their own reasons, an option that only 53 of the 505 respondents chose, indicating the validity of the motivations listed. A sample of such open-ended responses are as follows:

- To break [the] outgoing party's monopoly
- To raise awareness of beneficial alternatives to government policy of commercial incineration
- To promote socialism/class politics
- Lifelong ambition
- To increase women's participation
- Nearing retirement as teacher and seeking to change career
- I only entered the local elections as a joke
- To break large party control of council
- To get rid of councillors I felt had a conflict of interest
- To respect the disadvantaged
- To bring my own agenda and philosophy to public life
- To return local government to the people
- To highlight rural decline
- To keep someone else out
- Facilitated by changes in lifestyle circumstances
- To cost Fianna Fáil seats
- To change the system
- Passionate interest in fair play

One particular candidate admitted that he ran out of 'devilment' because he wanted 'to destroy a rival candidate of the same name'. His campaign platform also called for a full investigation into the assassination of Archduke Franz Ferdinand in 1914, the event which sparked off the First

World War.[5] It is our assumption that such candidates are few and far between. We also assume that most candidates seek to maximise their vote, regardless of their chances of victory. These candidates can then be subdivided into two broad categories based on their motivation for running, known formally in the academic literature as instrumental and expressive actors. The key difference between these categories is that for the first the outcome is the crucial matter (that is, winning a seat), while for the latter participation in the campaign is their ultimate gratification. To determine the strength of instrumental and expressive incentives amongst local election candidates, they were asked to rank the importance of each of the following factors as a motive for running. Their responses are detailed in the next two sections.

Instrumental incentives:

- Asked to run by a party
- To win a seat
- To represent one's local area
- To achieve certain policy goals

Expressive incentives:

- To highlight an important issue
- Asked to run by a group or organisation
- To continue family representation in political life
- Interested in politics

Instrumental incentives

A request, whether formally or informally, from someone in the party fold is a common reason explaining the emergence of candidates. Since one of the key functions of political parties is to recruit candidates for political office, this should come as no surprise. The vast majority of party candidates (68 per cent) state that such a request is quite important in their decision to run (see table 5.1 below). While the level of importance did vary between parties (more so for Sinn Féin, and less so for Labour and Green candidates), these differences are of limited size. The only group, not surprisingly, for whom this incentive is not a major factor is the 'others' category, the vast majority of whom comprise Independents and for whom this is a largely an irrelevant question. What

TABLE 5.1 IMPORTANCE OF 'ASKED TO RUN BY A PARTY' AS AN INCENTIVE IN RUNNING (%)

Party	Not at all important	Somewhat important	Quite important
Fianna Fáil	9	20	71
Fine Gael	12	22	66
Labour	21	14	65
Prog. Dems.	12	24	64
Green Party	17	21	62
Sinn Féin	8	9	83
Others	75	4	21

Note: In this and all other tables on candidates' incentives in this chapter, 'not at all important' refers to those answering with a score of between 1 and 3 on the scale of importance, 'somewhat important' to scores of between 4 and 6, and 'quite important' to scores of between 7 and 10.

Source: 2004 local election candidate survey, question 1.

would be interesting to read, but what candidates were not willing to reveal, was whether a party request is an open invitation or more a coded demand. It is worth noting that quite a few candidates hint at their running for the greater good of the party. Examples of such responses were: 'to basically help my party Fianna Fáil'; 'to maximise party vote'; and 'to pick up local personal vote to transfer to party colleague'. (The latter two quotes are from Fine Gael candidates.)

Possibly the foremost instrumental incentive is to win a seat, as this represents the purest form of self-ambition. Most party candidates are quite honest in this being a very important factor in their running. Looking at the respective proportions in table 5.2 below, it is most important for Fianna Fáil candidates (90 per cent), and least important for 'others'. The 'quite important' column indicates that the significance of this factor appears related to party size, and by implication, the possibility of winning a seat. While Fianna Fáil or Fine Gael candidates might therefore appear more ambitious than Green Party or 'other' candidates, this is more likely a realisation on their part of the strong possibility of their not winning a seat. Of course, it could just be that those who lost the election may feel impelled to underplay the importance of winning a seat. It must also be recognised that some do not simply seek to win a seat for their own sake, but also for the party. One such candidate wanted 'to strengthen [the] Labour Party and opposition to government', while a Sinn Féin candidate wanted 'to build party political strength'.

TABLE **5.2** IMPORTANCE OF 'TO WIN A SEAT' AS AN INCENTIVE IN RUNNING (%)

Party	Not at all important	Somewhat important	Quite important
Fianna Fáil	2	8	90
Fine Gael	9	7	84
Labour	9	11	80
Prog. Dems.	12	8	80
Green Party	9	18	73
Sinn Féin	10	14	76
Others	13	20	67

Source: 2004 local election candidate survey, question 1.

'All politics is local' said former Speaker of the US House of Representatives, Tip O'Neill, and at council elections, it is even more local than elsewhere. Localism is an undeniable feature of Irish politics, and most politicians, even party leaders, cannot afford to ignore its demands. The local Fianna Fáil organisation in Cavan did so to its cost in 1991 when it lost three seats to a local group (the Cavan Roads Action Group) concerned with the state of roads in the county. It is not surprising then that 90 per cent or more of Fianna Fáil, Fine Gael, Progressive Democrat and Green candidates cite representing their local area as quite an important factor in their decision to run. The specific reasons given include 'representing local people with local issues' (Independent); 'important to have strong worker in the area' (Fianna Fáil); 'to give better local representation' (Independent); 'to be a strong voice for my local area' (Progressive Democrat). Contrary to its image as a nationally oriented party, 100 per cent of Progressive Democrats surveyed cited this reason as 'quite important', while perhaps because of a focus on the 'national question', Sinn Féin candidates were least likely to report localism as an important factor in running. The differences between the party proportions are quite minor, however, and in most cases not statistically significant (which means they could be due to a random error resulting from our data comprising a sample); for the vast majority of candidates, representing the local area is an important incentive fuelling their candidacy. Indeed, only 25 of the 505 respondents said this was not important (of whom 12 still managed to win a seat). Despite the almost universal claim to be a local broker of sorts, this may not be the ultimate aim for all candidates. For some, representation of constituents, or to 'persecute civil servants',[6] may be their *raison d'être*. Others may have little appetite for these activities, but are using it as a means to an end (usually higher office). One Green candidate therefore said he 'wanted to build a base for the future'.

TABLE **5.3** IMPORTANCE OF 'TO REPRESENT LOCAL AREA' AS AN INCENTIVE IN RUNNING (%)

Party	Not at all important	Somewhat important	Quite important
Fianna Fáil	2	1	97
Fine Gael	7	3	90
Labour	10	9	81
Prog. Dems.	0	0	100
Green Party	5	5	90
Sinn Féin	5	24	71
Others	7	6	87

Source: 2004 local election candidate survey, question 1.

While for many politicians, their private instrumental incentive may be to win a seat, publicly they tend to declare more altruistic motives, of which one of the more common is to achieve policy objectives. Sinn Féin candidates (95 per cent of them) are more likely to cite this as an important factor in their running, while Fine Gael candidates are least likely to (although this lesser figure was still an impressive 73 per cent; see table 5.4). In all likelihood this reflects the policy-oriented nature of small parties, as the Progressive Democrats (at least prior to its termination), the Green Party and Sinn Féin are more focused on achieving policy goals than the centrist and mainstream Fianna Fáil, Fine Gael and Labour parties. There are a number of reasons for this divergence, one being that it is easier for small parties to have a few clear policy objectives; in contrast, the larger parties' policies become muddled as the realities of government formation dictate their having to produce a wider, and by implication, more of a compromise policy programme. Of course, the nature of these policies varies greatly, ranging from 'to get rid of corruption' to 'anti-war and environmental issues'. One Independent had the ambiguous aim of wanting to 'bring my own philosophy to public life'. We also have to question to what extent candidates are realistic about their ability to achieve these policy goals or whether it is a necessary ritual for them – that is, do candidates mention policies simply because they have to be seen to stand for something? The weak position of local government in the Irish political system means that it is not the ideal base from which to enact particular policies. We have to wonder to what extent candidates feel the need to offer a politically correct response and whether this masks their real intentions.

TABLE 5.4. IMPORTANCE OF 'TO ACHIEVE CERTAIN POLICY GOALS' AS AN INCENTIVE IN RUNNING (%)

Party	Not at all important	Somewhat important	Quite important
Fianna Fáil	8	9	83
Fine Gael	5	22	73
Labour	4	20	76
Prog. Dems.	0	13	87
Green Party	5	13	82
Sinn Féin	0	5	95
Others	9	13	78

Source: 2004 local election candidate survey, question 1.

Expressive incentives

For expressive actors, the action is more important than the outcome. An example of such an incentive is running a campaign to highlight an issue, be it the proposed closure of a local hospital or the proliferation of potholes. For such candidates, while winning a seat would undoubtedly benefit their cause, their aim is not directly linked to the result of the election. Such candidates participate to express their feelings on a matter; for example, if an individual is aggrieved over an issue, running at an election can be a convenient and relatively low-cost method of gaining publicity, which might otherwise be difficult and expensive to achieve. This is particularly the case for Independents, many of whom run out of annoyance over an issue. In 2004, this included candidates who wanted 'to highlight the importance of the constitution as the core legal document of

Ireland' and others who wanted 'to highlight rural decline'. Sometimes candidates are representatives of organisations (including those running on behalf of interest groups, such as the aforementioned 'hole-in-the-road gang' in Cavan or the Workers and Unemployed Action Group in Tipperary), or often they are running on their own initiative. Parties tend to avoid such candidates, because they usually run on a single issue, and often place this before the interests of the party. Individuals aggrieved over an issue therefore normally have to run as an Independent, and this can be the main reason why such candidates stand. The survey evidence backs this up, as 77 per cent of Independents said this is quite an important factor in their decision to run, compared to just 47 per cent of party candidates (calculated from table 5.5). Indeed, 55 per cent of Independents give this incentive the maximum score of ten on the scale of importance, in contrast to just 21 per cent of their party counterparts. In other words, those most concerned with highlighting an issue are more likely to run as an Independent (58 per cent) than for a party (42 per cent), a quite significant finding in itself. However, this does not imply that such individuals have the choice of either Independent or party status; rather the Independent ranks have more issue-oriented candidates. As stated above, approximately half of party candidates cite an issue as a major factor in running, but this proportion is higher amongst both Green (59 per cent) and Sinn Féin (67 per cent) candidates – again evidence of the policy-oriented nature of these parties.

TABLE **5.5** IMPORTANCE OF 'TO HIGHLIGHT AN IMPORTANT ISSUE' AS
AN INCENTIVE IN RUNNING

Party	Not at all important	Somewhat important	Quite important
Fianna Fáil	27	25	48
Fine Gael	32	25	43
Labour	35	25	40
Prog. Dems.	32	23	45
Green Party	18	23	59
Sinn Féin	22	11	67
Others	13	11	76

Source: 2004 local election candidate survey, question 1.

When an organisation, for example an interest group or local community association, wishes to highlight its concern or grievance over an issue, it sometimes runs a candidate to promote its cause, or one runs to facilitate the group's representation. While the issues are predominantly local in nature, examples in 2004 being the Naas Planning Alliance (opposed to haphazard building developments) and a variety of anti-incinerator groups, there are the occasional interest groups mobilised for other reasons. Notable examples occur in the border counties, including the Donegal Progressive Party and the Monaghan Protestant Association. Both of these groups fielded (and elected) candidates for a number of decades up to the 1990s. What distinguishes interest groups in Ireland from those in other political systems is that firstly, they are willing to enter the political process by fielding election candidates (in a study of twelve different single-issue protest campaigns in Britain, only two fielded candidates at an election),[7] and secondly, these candidates sometimes win a seat. Because they aim to mobilise support across party and socio-economic divisions, as well as ensuring that their candidates are seen to be outside the political establishment, interest groups tend to support, or even nominate, Independent candidates. One example is the Roscommon Hospital Action Committee, which ran three Independents in 2004, continuing a policy of contesting every general and local election since 1985. Over 39 per cent of Independents (and others) say that a request from a group or organisation is quite an important factor in their decision to run (see table 5.6 below), in contrast to the considerably lower mean figure (which admittedly is quite a high figure in itself) of 25 per cent of party candidates. This average holds constant across most of the parties, although it is less important for Labour – surprisingly, given its affiliation with

TABLE **5.6** IMPORTANCE OF 'ASKED TO RUN BY A GROUP/ORGANISATION' AS AN INCENTIVE IN RUNNING (%)

Party	Not at all important	Somewhat important	Quite important
Fianna Fáil	60	14	26
Fine Gael	59	19	22
Labour	73	11	16
Prog. Dems.	65	10	25
Green Party	68	5	27
Sinn Féin	44	11	45
Others	48	13	39

Source: 2004 local election candidate survey, question 1.

trade unions – and more important for Sinn Féin candidates. Unfortunately, details concerning the nature of the groups to which candidates were affiliated were not obtained, although one suspects that in the majority of cases these comprise local residents' or community associations.

Political family dynasties, sometimes present in other liberal democracies (examples being the Kennedy and Bush families in the United States), have been to a much greater extent a recurring feature of Irish political life. The notion of a family 'holding onto a seat' may seem something of a paradox in a democracy, where it is the public who have the power of election, yet there are countless examples of seats being 'passed on' from generation to generation, as local electorates remain loyal to a family name. Such candidates may not necessarily run just to retain a seat within their family, but a history of political activity by previous generations stirs up interest and creates an incentive for them to run. Consequently, while this motive may be considered instrumental, for the purposes of this study it is categorised as expressive. The rationale is that successive generations of family members may be more concerned with maintaining a family presence in politics rather than achieving some specific political outcomes. For example, when recounting her decision to first run for local office, Marcella Corcoran-Kennedy, a Fine Gael councillor in Offaly, cited no burning desire to influence policy or represent the locality. Instead she referred to her status as the eldest child of a former county councillor, and the granddaughter of one before him.[8] Fianna Fáil and 'other' candidates are more likely to cite familial representation as an incentive in running than those from other parties, while this factor is least important for Labour candidates. Three in every ten candidates from either Fianna Fáil or Fine Gael state that this motive is either somewhat or quite important, three times the proportion of Labour candidates expressing a similar sentiment. It seems that dynastic politics is a more significant feature within the civil war parties, and this was especially evident in 2004 because of the ban on holding a dual mandate. A considerable proportion of TDs who resigned their council seats between 2002 and 2004 ensured the co-opting of a relative into their seat. This protected the TDs from the emergence of new rivals, and also ensured they kept a local ear to the ground. Consequently, many of these co-opted relatives ran in 2004. Examples include Eleanor Roche (wife of junior minister Dick Roche) in Wicklow County Council, Gary O'Flynn in Cork City Council (son of Noel O'Flynn) and Seán Sherlock, also in Cork County

TABLE **5.7** IMPORTANCE OF 'TO CONTINUE FAMILY REPRESENTATION IN POLITICAL LIFE' AS AN INCENTIVE IN RUNNING (%)

Party	Not at all important	Somewhat important	Quite important
Fianna Fáil	68	5	27
Fine Gael	71	15	14
Labour	89	4	7
Prog. Dems.	76	9	15
Green Party	84	4	12
Sinn Féin	81	6	13
Others	73	3	24

Source: 2004 local election candidate survey, question 1.

Council (son of Joe Sherlock). All told, thirty councillors running in 2004 had been co-opted in place of a family relative who resigned because of the dual mandate ban. Fifteen of these co-opted councillors ran for Fianna Fáil, three for Fine Gael and six for Labour (source: electionsireland.org).

Another expressive incentive is that some individuals are 'political animals'. This motivates them to become politically active, whether in an interest group or a party. The late Independent TD Tony Gregory began his political life as a councillor representing the North Centre City Community Action Project (NCCCAP). His motivation for entering the electoral arena was quite simple: he wanted to be a political activist.[9] Of course, many who are politically active do not run for office, so a key question is why do some opt for this route? Some candidates claim they were pushed into this position. Although he is an example from the national level, the previously mentioned Tom Gildea was just such a reluctant candidate for the Dáil elections in 1997. Representing an interest group in Donegal mobilised over the retention of a television deflector in the region, he was elected as its spokesperson, but maintained a very low political profile. After Gildea secured a resolution of the deflector issue from Bertie Ahern's minority government, he did not seek re-election to the Dáil and disappeared from the national political limelight.

Some political activists may conclude that they have a greater chance to be influential from within the system. For others the taste of politics may be insatiable: contesting public elections might therefore be the next logical step. One such Progressive Democrat candidate said he ran in 2004 because he was 'already active in a local community organisation'; his appetite had been whetted. For such candidates, it is the excitement generated by the campaign that impels them to run, with the outcome being of secondary importance. Of course, a desire for political activism can be quite distinct from an interest in politics, which could be more concerned with debating lofty ideals and philosophies. Nevertheless, this chapter is focused on determining candidates' interests, and perhaps not surprisingly, on average 88 per cent of party candidates and 74 per cent of Independents cited their interest in politics as an important incentive in running (see table 5.8). It is extremely doubtful that this is these candidates' sole, or indeed primary, motive to run. However, it is expected that those who contest elections exhibit high levels of interest in politics, and it is also a non-controversial incentive to select in a survey, in contrast to more personal ambition-related factors. Fianna Fáil candidates seem to be more motivated by

TABLE 5.8 IMPORTANCE OF 'INTERESTED IN POLITICS' AS AN INCENTIVE IN RUNNING (%)

Party	Not at all important	Somewhat important	Quite important
Fianna Fáil	2	4	94
Fine Gael	4	6	90
Labour	0	16	84
Prog. Dems.	4	13	83
Green Party	9	4	87
Sinn Féin	0	15	85
Others	10	18	72

Source: 2004 local election candidate survey, question 1.

this factor than their counterparts in the smaller parties, particularly Sinn Féin or the Green Party. Nevertheless, the high proportion of candidates incentivised by interest across all the parties means that we should not read too much into these differences, many of which are not statistically significant.

How do these incentives fare relative to one another? The average score per party on the 1–10 scale of importance for each of the eight incentives to run is detailed in table 5.9 below. These incentives are ranked according to their importance to the mean party candidate. The highest average score across party candidates was 8.8 for 'to represent local area', while the lowest score was 3.2 for 'to continue family representation in political life'. What is interesting is that most of the expressive incentives (detailed in italics) prop up the table, while instrumental incentives are far more important. This indicates that party candidates motivations' in running are more to do with achieving a particular outcome rather than a gratification from participation in the political process. This does not mean that the latter is not important for party candidates, but it may well be a realisation that gratification can be furthered when linked to a certain outcome. This pattern is generally repeated across the party groupings, but there are some exceptions. All of the parties (bar Fine Gael) rank 'to achieve certain policy goals' above 'asked to run by a party', while the former incentive is more important than 'to win a seat' for the Green Party, Sinn Féin and 'others'. The motivations of 'others', and in particular Independents, appear slightly different from party candidates. Achieving certain policy goals and highlighting important issues are more significant incentives for Independents, as is being asked to run by a group or organisation. This confirms the more policy- and issue-oriented nature of Independents that is often portrayed in the media.

TABLE 5.9. MEAN IMPORTANCE OF INCENTIVES

Incentive	Fianna Fáil	Fine Gael	Labour	Prog. Dems	Green Party	Sinn Féin	Oth.	All Cands.
To represent local area	9.2	8.6	8.3	9.6	8.5	8.3	8.7	8.8
Interested in politics	9.0	8.6	8.5	8.0	8.3	8.8	7.8	8.6
To win a seat	7.7	8.3	8.4	8.1	7.8	7.9	7.6	8.2
Asked to run by a party	7.7	7.3	6.9	7.3	6.8	8.2	3.0	8.2
To achieve certain policy goals	8.0	7.6	7.9	8.2	8.4	8.9	8.1	8.0
To highlight important issue	5.7	5.7	5.3	5.7	6.8	7.1	7.9	5.9
Asked to run by group or organisation	3.8	3.7	2.9	3.4	3.4	4.8	4.8	3.7
To continue family representation	3.7	2.9	1.8	2.7	1.9	2.3	3.2	3.2

Note: These figures are the mean score of importance given to each incentive on a scale of 1 to 10, where 1 means 'not at all important' and 10 means 'extremely important'. The figures in italics refer to expressive incentives, while those in normal text are instrumental incentives.
Source: 2004 local election candidate survey, question 1.

While most motivations are covered by these eight umbrella incentives, there are undoubtedly other factors outside of this framework, some of them specific to particular types of candidates. For example, owing to both the strong non-partisan nature of local elections and the non-partisan nature of their candidacies, some Independents might be motivated to run by anti-party sentiment. Indeed, while no party candidates expressed anti-party sentiment in the sample of literature examined (hardly a surprise), 24 per cent of Independents made negative comments about party politics, examples of such statements including:

- It is time to give party politics the boot.
- Any local councillor, or TD, who is a member of a party, cannot fully represent you properly.
- Can you trust the political parties any more?
- Once again the Political Parties, and their Public Representatives, have failed our Community.
- The political parties have no answer to the situation [regarding problems in society] and are often the worst example to those in deprived circumstances.

Other reasons to run for office that were listed in a study of local councillors in Britain include 'power, status, self-aggrandisement, ambition, compensation for personal insecurity, or even sexual inadequacy'.[10] The power aspect should certainly not be ignored, as it is undoubtedly a major influencing factor for potential candidates. While local councillors may be considered by some to have no real power, they can have an influential say on some local policies, planning being a historical example. This power also stems from the status associated with holding political office. It has been claimed that working-class councillors 'who failed to realise their intellectual potential during their education and therefore have jobs which they find insufficiently interesting or demanding' are particularly inclined to seek local office.[11] They may wish to compensate for a personal insecurity arising from their low-status occupation: for such candidates local office offers the potential of an alternative and parallel career. To this extent, the prestige arising from being a councillor is not related to an objective evaluation of the power of the position, but 'the prestige it brings to the councillor in his own eyes'.[12] A British report on the management of local government in the 1960s cited something similar, asserting that younger councillors in more interesting jobs saw council work as a *supplement,* middle-aged councillors in more mundane jobs saw it as *compensation,* while retired councillors see it as a *substitute.*[13]

One possible, although probably not plausible, factor explaining candidate motivation is financial gain. While one candidate said he ran because he was 'nearing retirement as a teacher and seeking to change career', this is more the case of someone running as an aforementioned substitute for their work. As detailed in chapter 2, the financial remuneration from the state for councillors has historically been very low. While the details of corruption in Dublin County Council emanating from the Flood and Mahon tribunals indicate that some councillors profited from their position, it is unlikely that a desire for ill-gotten gain is a motive for any candidate. There are far easier and more reliable means of earning an income by corrupt methods. It is more probable that the attraction of bribery for the guilty individuals concerned is only something that emerged once they were in a position to turn a blind eye. As for the sexual inadequacy motive, it is beyond the scope of this book to assess its importance. However, what this motive reveals is how difficult it can be to understand candidates' true private intentions. The full range listed from the British study detailed above are incentives that we may well recognise, but which can be very difficult to both measure and identify. While some claim that it is quite obvious that those running for political office are concerned with power, prestige and self-aggrandisement, there are a lot of individuals who seek these goals via a different avenue, one outside politics. In fact, most people who seek these aims choose not to run for political office. Why then does a relative handful do so? While the previous pages have detailed the relevance of a number of general incentives, personal motivation is a very difficult concept to study from a scientific manner; this explains why there have been relatively few studies of candidates' psychological traits.

Sociological Model

Having assessed some of the direct incentives explaining candidate emergence at local elections, this section tests the veracity of the sociological model. This predicts that candidates' decision to run is a function of their socio-economic background. Applying this model, it is unlikely that we will find results that predict exactly whether an individual will run for election for a particular party; however, the aim of this section is find out whether there are any characteristics particular to party candidates that distinguish them from first, the wider electorate, and second, from each other.

The main problem with this model is that for most candidates, running for office is not a simple choice of picking whatever party one fancies (although exceptions do exist, particularly in the case of 'celebrity' names. An example at the national level such as Tom Parlon comes to mind: having served as president of the Irish Farmers' Association, he sought to enter politics at the 2002 election, and was heavily courted by both Fine Gael and the Progressive Democrats). Ultimately, this decision rests with the party and its officers, a decision which is heavily influenced by a potential candidate's history of involvement with a party. Years of association with a particular party, therefore, can increase the probability of being picked as a candidate by that party, but it can concurrently diminish the odds of being picked by any other party – in the unlikely scenario that it was sought. This problem means that we need to be wary of our findings, because the outcome – that is, the particular candidates picked – may not be the result of a certain type of candidate being attracted to a party, but because the party sought only this type of candidate – perhaps in order to maintain a specific profile. The rest of this section compares the socio-economic characteristics of candidates and voters. The data for voters comes from the 2002 Irish National Election Study.[14]

Socio-economic characteristics

Beginning with candidates' age, survey respondents were asked only their year of birth, so without knowing the exact date, what follows is a very close estimation of their age, which at most could be a year out. The average party candidate was aged 48 in 2004, slightly older than voters (47), although not a statistically significant difference. Candidates for Sinn Féin (a mean age of 42), the Progressive Democrats (45) and the Green Party (47) were slightly younger than those from Fianna Fáil (50), Fine Gael (50) or Labour (49). Table 5.11 also subdivides the candidates per age category. There are very few candidates from the 18 to 24 category: as few as 4 per cent of Fianna Fáil, Labour and Progressive Democrat candidates fall within this age range, while there are none from this group in either the Green or Sinn Féin ranks. When 12 per cent of voters are aged under 25, it may explain why turnout is lower amongst young people relative to other age sectors. Most candidates (almost two-thirds) fall within the 25 to 44 category; it might be expected that candidates at local elections are slightly younger than those at general elections simply because running at the former is often a precursor to an attempt at the latter. Close to one-third of candidates are in the 45 to 64 age category, while there are few pensioners running for any party. Since approximately 17 per cent of voters are pensioners, this weakens the validity of the hypothesis about young voters that lack of representation discourages turnout; after all, more than 75 per cent of pensioners voted in the 2002 general election.[15]

TABLE 5.10 SOCIO-ECONOMIC BACKGROUND OF CANDIDATES
AND VOTERS

	Fianna Fáil	Fine Gael	Labour	Prog. Dems.	Green Party	Sinn Féin	Other Cand.	Voter
AGE (MEAN)	50	50	49	45	47	42	51	47
AGE GROUPING								
18–24	**4**	8	**4**	**4**	0	0	**5**	12
25–44	**63**	**59**	**70**	42	67	52	**65**	36
45–64	31	32	**23**	54	25	43	27	36
65+	**2**	**1**	**2**	0	8	**4**	**2**	17
SEX								
Male	**87**	**83**	**82**	79	67	**85**	**88**	49
Female	**13**	**17**	**18**	21	33	**15**	**12**	51
ORGANISATIONAL MEMBERSHIP AT TIME OF ELECTION								
Community/ residents' assoc.	34	41	44	54	42	50	42	n/a
IFA/farming assoc.	18	19	6	8	0	0	10	n/a
GAA	**44**	**33**	8	23	8	**33**	17	16
Trade union	**5**	**12**	33	4	21	13	**15**	33
Professional org.	13	10	**4**	8	13	**4**	7	16
CLASS								
White collar	38	**32**	33	31	54	**17**	29	50
Self-employed	**15**	9	6	19	17	0	11	6
Skilled	10	13	19	15	4	29	13	11
Semi- & unskilled	**3**	**4**	13	**4**	0	8	9	24
Farmers	**22**	19	**2**	15	0	0	11	9
OTHER								
Third level education	45	**51**	67	65	92	39	49	28
Rural area or village	47	44	**19**	35	**33**	21	40	44
Large town or city	**32**	**38**	54	50	54	46	37	48
N	96	94	48	26	24	24	193	2,654

Note: Age refers to the average age of each category. All other figures are proportions within each party exhibiting that particular trait. Figures in bold note candidate characteristics different from voters at a statistically significant level of 0.05 (that is, there is a one-in-twenty possibility of these findings being due to chance).

N refers to the numbers within each category.

Source: author's analysis of 2004 local election candidate survey.

Data on voters comes from Marsh et al, 2008.

In terms of gender, the profile of the candidates in 2004 followed a tradition of under-representation of women in Irish politics, as 84 per cent of all candidates were male. The Progressive Democrats and the Green Party were more successful in their aspirations for gender equality, as women comprised 21 per cent of candidates for the former and 33 per cent for the latter. The respective figures for Fianna Fáil, Fine Gael and Labour were a lowly 13, 17 and 18 per cent. Despite an express desire for more female candidates within Fianna Fáil and Fine Gael (in the case of the former, one-third of all candidates by 2014), it is likely that swift change will only result from the implementation of gender quotas. For the 2009 local elections, both Labour and Sinn Féin adopted 30 per cent quotas, and the Green Party a 40 per cent quota. Perhaps because of a failure to reach the party's target of 33 per cent female candidacies in 2004, Labour also adopted a mentoring programme for 2009 whereby senior female politicians provide assistance to some of its new candidates.

Involvement in the community and/or local organisations can also influence one to participate in politics. For example, if individuals are members of a local residents' association or a community group, this can socialise them into becoming a political animal, and if they seek even more political activity, the next rational step might then be to run for office. Table 5.10 above shows the importance of group membership as 41 per cent of party candidates belong to a local community or residents' association. Both Sinn Féin (50 per cent) and Progressive Democrat (54 per cent) candidates are more likely to be members of such organisations than their counterparts from Fianna Fáil (34 per cent). In contrast, most candidates who are members of a farming association run for either Fianna Fáil or Fine Gael. GAA membership is an important asset for Fianna Fáil, Fine Gael and Sinn Féin candidates as the proportion of their candidates affiliated to the organisation is twice the proportion within the electorate. The GAA seems less relevant to Labour and Green Party candidates, with only 8 per cent of them being members. While one-third of the population are affiliated to trade unions, significantly fewer candidates are. Only Labour exhibits a similar level of membership, while as few as 5 per cent of Fianna Fáil and 4 per cent of Progressive Democrat candidates belong to trade unions.

In line with findings from other studies, candidates, being a political elite, had achieved a higher level of education than the public, with 53 per cent having some form of third-level education, in contrast to 28 per cent of voters. A strikingly large proportion of candidates from some of the small parties have such a qualification: 92 per cent of Green Party, 67 per cent of Labour and 65 per cent of Progressive Democrat candidates. Neither Sinn Féin nor candidates from the 'others' category have such high levels of education and this is probably a reflection of the middle-class profile of the three aforementioned parties. Of the two mainstream parties, Fianna Fáil are slightly less educated with 45 per cent of their candidates in possession of a third-level qualification, in contrast to 51 per cent of Fine Gael candidates.

There is a clear territorial bias in the profile of some of the parties' candidates. Only one-fifth of both Labour and Sinn Féin's candidates live in the countryside, probably due to the simple fact that these parties – which have a particular urban profile – run fewer candidates in such areas. Almost 50 per cent of Fianna Fáil and Fine Gael candidates live in the countryside, a figure that falls to approximately one-third of Progressive Democrat and Green Party candidates. As is the case at general elections, the two civil war parties dominate political representation in rural areas.

The last, and often the most important, socio-economic variable is the occupation or class profile of the candidates. The Green Party has the most middle-class profile of all the parties as none of its candidates are recruited from either traditional blue-collar or farming backgrounds. Labour (13 per cent) and Sinn Féin (9 per cent) have the highest working-class representation, but a stark feature of political life is that very few blue-collar workers run for office. Most self-employed candidates generally run under the Fianna Fáil, Progressive Democrat and Green Party mantles, perhaps an acknowledgement of something in these parties' policies that attracts this type of candidate. Finally, the vast majority of farming candidates run for either Fianna Fáil or Fine Gael. Somewhat surprisingly, 15 per cent of Progressive Democrat candidates also come from a farming background, although this may be testament to the recruiting skills of Tom Parlon, the party's TD at the time (and former IFA president) in Laois–Offaly.

Other Factors

While the previous sections assessed the importance of candidates' personal characteristics in explaining their emergence, this decision is also affected by external factors. These include:

- the level of resources available to candidates
- the nomination process
- the electoral rules
- the level of competition

Because the average amount spent by candidates at local elections in 2004 is the rather small sum of €3,000 (see chapter 6), this indicates that resources should not be a key factor. However, candidates also need to take into account the opportunity costs of working as an elected local representative, something that can have a detrimental effect on their income, particularly in the case of those already in a reasonably paid career. The nomination process determines the openness of the system. Party candidates are affected by the demands a party may place on them; for example, a record of membership with the party is usually required. Those running for Fianna Fáil in 2009 had to put themselves before an interview panel, something that may not appeal to some potential candidates. The level of control exercised by both the local organisation and local councillors on the process also affects the openness of the system. To minimise competition, some councillors may do their utmost to prevent candidates emerging within their party, particularly if they wield a significant influence over the local party branches. The level of democratisation within the party is therefore an important factor for candidates to consider. Where the one-member, one-vote (OMOV) system is in use for selection conventions candidates have a greater opportunity of securing a nomination than under the traditional delegate-based system. With the exception of Fianna Fáil, all parties are now using OMOV to select their candidates.

Outside of parties, three aspects of the official nomination process that Independents have to consider are: the number of signatures required to support a candidacy, the size of the deposit, and the proportion of the vote needed for it to be refunded. Looking at these factors for national elections, one comparative study examined the ease of access to run as a candidate across eighteen industrial democracies.[16] Ireland was described as the third least cartelised system (after Luxembourg and Denmark). While this should encourage more individuals to seek a nomination for general elections in Ireland, this hypothesis does not hold for local elections, where the comparative restrictions tend to be eased. In the UK, for example, to contest a general election, candidates need the signatures of ten registered voters and a €750 deposit. At local elections, no deposit is required. Regardless of the comparative ranking of ease of access in Ireland, because most countries have some kind of requirement to run for office, it is difficult to imagine a much more open system than the Irish case. Under the Electoral Amendment Bill 2008, it is proposed that candidates will need only a €100 deposit to run for city or council election (€50 for any other local elections) or the signatures of fifteen voters.

The other two factors affecting candidates are interrelated: the electoral system and the level of competition in the constituency. The former, PR-STV, can have a positive influence on the emergence of candidates. The presence of multi-seat constituencies under PR-STV reduces the number of safe seats, so often a feature of plurality systems such as in the UK or France. In these countries, this has discouraged potential candidates to the extent that uncontested seats were until recently a regular feature of these electoral landscapes. The candidate-centred nature of PR-STV can also act as an inducement to candidates, because it facilitates a personalistic style of competition that does not necessarily revolve around party loyalties. Consequently, those from outside the main parties (Independents in particular) are at less of a disadvantage than is the case under a party-centred electoral system. While PR-STV has a significant influence on the level of electoral competition, a related factor is the number of seats on offer. Put simply, the more offices there are to be filled, the more opportunities there are for candidates to run. The results in table 5.11 below indicate that, from a comparative perspective, there are far fewer local government positions in Ireland than elsewhere in the European Union. With 36,700 communes, France has a local council for every 1,600 of its citizens and an elected member for every 118. Austria has one *gemeinden* (local council) per 3,500 people and one councillor per 209. At the other extreme, the average population per council in Ireland is 33,000 with one councillor for every 2,336 persons. Only the UK has a higher ratio of councillors to population than Ireland. It is therefore more difficult to win local office in Ireland than in other European countries because there are more potential candidates within each constituency.

TABLE **5.11** COUNCIL AND COUNCILLOR REPRESENTATION IN THE
EUROPEAN UNION

Country	Population (millions)	No. of local councils	Average pop. per council	Avg. size of council	Pop. per cllr.
France	59.6	36,700	1,600	14	118
Austria	8.2	2,350	3,500	17	209
Sweden	8.8	310	28,400	111*	256
Germany	83	15,300	5,400	15	350
Finland	5.2	452	11,500	28	410
Italy	57.7	8,100	7,100	12	608
Spain	40	8,100	4,900	8	610
Belgium	10.3	589	17,500	22	811
Greece	10.6	1,033	10,300	10	1,075
Denmark	5.4	275	19,600	17	1,115
Portugal	10.1	308	32,800	29	1,131
Netherlands	16	548	29,000	19	1,555
Ireland	4	114	35,000	14	2,500
UK	59.6	468	127,350	49	2,603

Source: Hughes et al, 2007, p. 517.
* Includes deputies, elected at the same time.

Conclusion

This chapter has looked at why some people decide to run
as candidates at local elections. To understand their motives,
a straightforward open-ended question could have been
used in the candidate survey, but this would probably have
resulted in 'safe', politically correct and idiosyncratic
responses that would have shed little new light on candidate
emergence. Instead, this chapter has explored a number of
methods to determine candidate incentives. It was found

that most candidates are quite instrumental in their reasons for running, but this begs another question: given the limited authority vested in local government, what did these individuals hope to achieve? The sociological model demonstrated that candidates possess the typical characteristics of those who run for office in other systems: they are more likely to be male, middle-aged and well-educated. However, this model is extremely limited because it just predicts that those with certain characteristics are more likely to run than others – not that all, or indeed only, these candidates will have these characteristics. Most middle-aged, well-educated males never consider running for office. This suggests that candidates are motivated or inspired by something else. Power, prestige, self-aggrandisement and sexual inadequacy have all been cited, but this would require a psychological analysis of not just candidates, but also those who choose not to run. For example, a finding that the majority of candidates run to compensate a self-perceived failure in other aspects of their personal lives would be interesting only if it was compared to the proportion of the population at large expressing such feelings of inadequacy.

Within the academic literature, it is suggested that there are particular types of characters who occupy local office. Categories identified range from the 'grievance-chaser', 'policy-maker', 'messenger boy', 'watchdog', 'delegate' to 'facilitators'.[17] However, these are not necessarily applicable to local *candidates* because the aforementioned are roles that evolve while in office. Nevertheless, this study has indicated the presence of a number of types of candidates. First is the *aspirant,* someone not that interested in local office, but who sees it as a useful route to national politics. Second is the *local broker*, someone looking to represent and fight for the interests of his or her local community. Third is the self-explanatory category of the *policy-maker*. Fourth is the *lobbyist*, a candidate running to promote the cause of an interest group. Fifth is the *activist*, an individual who enjoys politics and likes to devote their time to it. Sixth is the *loyalist*, someone not particularly keen on electoral office but runs because of a party request. Seventh is the *protector*; they run because of familial links to a politician, either to maintain a tradition of family representation or to 'protect' a local seat when a relative transfers to the national arena. Eighth is the *dissident*; their motivation stems from their falling out with an organisation over an issue, be it a party or a local community group. Outside of these eight categories is the *maverick*; their presence in the electoral contest is unpredictable and can be a product of idiosyncratic factors. This classification is based on the actual analysis of candidates' motives as opposed to a speculation about their private incentives. A typology based on the latter would surely produce a number of other types of candidates, but in the absence of hard evidence, this path is avoided for now.

Finally, if we consider the impact of the electoral arena on candidates, there has not been any great change in the power of local government since the foundation of the state, so it is not unreasonable to expect that the motives detailed here have not changed greatly across elections. The ban on a dual mandate has meant that there should be fewer candidates running for blatantly political reasons (i.e. TDs), but since many such TDs have had a relation step into the breach for them, there are still some running for local office simply to protect a local bailiwick. For example, in the candidate survey some said that their intention in running was 'to hold the seat that was here for thirty years' or 'to support an existing seat'. If local representatives were given more power, we might expect such attitudes to alter as candidates come to realise the importance of local office in its own right, not just as a stepping stone. While this chapter has detailed the motives and background of candidates, the next step is to assess what they do once the decision to run has been taken. With this in mind, the next chapter looks at the campaigns of local election candidates, namely what they do, and whether such efforts have an impact on the electorate.

6

Local Election Campaigns

This chapter examines what candidates do during their local election campaigns, and whether these campaigns have any effect. Campaigning is an important part of the political process because it is the period when candidates and the political system as a whole have a greater than usual visual presence. Both parties and politicians are under greater scrutiny during this period from the media and the public, with the former two bodies consequently devoting a lot of resources to their campaign efforts. The aim of this chapter is to detail what exactly these efforts consist of, and to determine whether it is a wise investment of energy. Following a brief discussion of campaigns, the data from the 2004 candidate survey is analysed to portray a picture of what goes on at local elections in Ireland.

Campaigns – what are they all about?

Campaigns have been described as 'organised efforts to inform, persuade and mobilise',[1] with the ultimate aim being to maximise electoral gains. While some candidates may be more interested in promoting policies than seeking office (especially, perhaps, Independents more so than party candidates – as was shown in the last chapter), if they fail to attract sufficient levels of votes, neither of these goals is likely to be achieved. Consequently, an assumption of this chapter is that almost all candidates will strive for the best electoral performance possible no matter what incentives they are primarily concerned with. This comes with the tacit acknowledgement of vote management, which entails candidates seeking only a quota of votes to ensure an equal distribution of party support, thus maximising the number of seats won.

Many comparative studies of campaigns argue that the nature of the effort involved has changed a great deal.[2] The evolution of campaigning has been grouped into three different eras according to their rate of 'modernism'.[3] In the 'pre-modern' era, campaigning was short-term and decentralised; local party branches organised their own independent campaigns with little direction from party headquarters. From the 1950s on, this style changed as campaigning became 'modernised': long-term campaigns centralised from national headquarters became the norm, with the importance of the localised element greatly reduced. Further changes in electioneering since the 1990s have given rise to what some have called 'the postmodern era', which entails a permanent campaign strictly controlled from the centre. A key debate to which this chapter contributes is to trace the element of modernism in Irish local election campaigns and to determine to what extent campaigning is more than a mere ritual. Focusing on the latter, campaigns have often been undertaken as a force of habit, sometimes simply due to enthusiasm for campaigning on the part of the grass-roots members. To this extent, a classic study on campaigns in the US found that its main influence was reinforcement, not conversion, because those who read most of the communication's output were those who had their political predispositions most firmly entrenched, whereas those most open to conversion were the least likely to pay heed to the campaign.[4]

Up until the late 1970s in Ireland, election outcomes (both local and general) were regarded by parties as either 'foregone conclusion[s]', where the national campaign had little effect, or were dependent on local campaigns.[5] Irish voters appeared fairly stable in their preferences, deciding their vote largely on the record of the incumbent government. Consequently the parties saw little point in wasting their limited resources on a forlorn attempt to persuade voters to change their minds at the ballot box. There was little to no long-term planning put into campaigns, with most strategies devised after the calling of an election.[6] As a result, campaigns were pretty much nondescript affairs that did not seek to capture the imagination of the Irish voter. For example, Cumann na nGaedheal initially favoured being entirely removed from local elections as a party organisation. The attitude of all parties towards local elections was never altogether favourable, as evidenced by the frequent postponing of polling dates. Such elections were viewed as an inconvenient distraction, particularly given the unitary, centralised nature of Irish government, where all policy emanated from the centre. The results of local elections changed little, so parties preferred to devote their limited resources to general elections; the consequence was that much of the campaigning was candidate-engineered. Broadly speaking, two types of candidates contested local elections: those using it as a first rung on the ladder to political office, and those who had already made it, but retained local office to keep an eye both on their constituency and any potential electoral rivals. It is this focus on candidates to which parties devoted most of their attention at local elections. To this extent, party campaigns at local elections are usually conducted in the context of the next general election – that is, they are used as a training ground to prepare for the more important national poll. Garret FitzGerald's use of the 1979 local elections to launch new candidates for Fine Gael is a notable example, and it undoubtedly contributed to the party's successes at the three general elections in the 1981–82 period.

Measuring the impact of campaign activity

Determining the impact of a campaign requires the identification of a number of key factors. In a study of electioneering in the UK, seven main components of a local election campaign were identified: preparation, organisation, election workers, canvassing, literature, use of computers, and polling day operations.[7] Using this as a framework, it can be seen that there are three general elements to a campaign:

1. The preparing and planning of a campaign
2. The level of campaign resources available to a candidate
3. The activities carried out during a campaign

Using data from the same 2004 survey of local election candidates as analysed in the previous chapter, the following sections assess the effort invested by candidates into the different aspects of a campaign, and ultimately, whether it made a difference to the outcome.

Preparation

Candidates were asked three questions about their campaign preparation: when they decided to run for election (in terms of how long before polling day), the length of their active campaign, and how far advanced their preparations for the campaign were (on a scale of 0 to 10, where 0 denotes 'no preparation', and 10 'all preparation was completed') when the election was officially called four weeks before polling day.

TABLE **6.1** LEVEL OF CAMPAIGN PREPARATION PER CANDIDATE

Party	When decided to run (time before election)	Active campaign length (months)	Campaign preparation
Fianna Fáil	2 yrs 2 mths	3.5	7.2
Fine Gael	1 yr 7 mths	3.7	7.5
Labour	1 yr 10 mths	4.0	7.3
Prog. Dems.	1 yr 4 mths	3.3	6.4
Green Party	1 yr 3 mths	3.5	6.0
Sinn Féin	1 yr 10 mths	4.0	7.5
Others	1 yr 4 mths	2.3	5.6

Source: 2004 local election candidate survey, question 5.

We can see from table 6.1 that Fianna Fáil candidates are the first off the mark in terms of deciding when to run. This is in part due to the party having the most incumbents who automatically plan to run again once elected. This may reflect an element of the aforementioned 'postmodernism', as permanent campaigns are a feature of such a phase of electioneering. Labour and Sinn Féin candidates are next off the mark, deciding to run twenty months before the election. Not surprisingly, given their lack of resources, Independents are the last into the political fray. This is also because it is a decision they can make on their own – in contrast to party candidates whose earlier decisions may have been influenced by the timing of selection conventions or pressure from party headquarters. Interestingly, in table 6.1 there is a very weak relationship between the timing of candidates' decision to run and the length of their active campaigns. Despite deciding to run over two years before the 2004 election, the average length of a Fianna Fáil candidate's campaign is three and a half months. Most candidates for all the parties run a campaign of similar length, while Independents run the shortest campaigns, at just over two months. In spite of their short campaigns, candidates are reasonably confident about their levels of preparation as most feel that the vast majority of preparation is completed when the election is officially called by the Minister for the Environment, Heritage and Local Government. It is only Independents who cram half their campaign preparation into the last few weeks before polling day.

Campaign resources

Candidates' level of campaign activity is generally dependent on the resources available to them, with the three foremost being: a campaign team, a personal computer, and an electoral register.

Campaign team

A traditional pre-modern campaign resource is a team of workers to carry out various thankless tasks, ranging from the sealing of envelopes to knocking on doors. As table 6.2 below details, Sinn Féin has the most daily helpers (six) and the largest campaign team (thirty-eight). Green candidates have the smallest campaign team, on average two per day and thirteen in total. Candidates from the other parties have an average-sized campaign team of thirty to pick from, of whom they have between five and seven helpers per day

TABLE **6.2** NUMBER OF DAILY AND TOTAL CAMPAIGN
HELPERS PER CANDIDATE

Party	Daily team (no. of helpers)	Total team (no. of helpers)
Fianna Fáil	6	34
Fine Gael	5	29
Labour	5	24
Prog. Dems.	7	28
Green Party	2	13
Sinn Féin	10	38
Others	6	24

Source: 2004 local election candidate survey, questions 6 and 7.

assisting them on the campaign trail. It is assessed later in this chapter whether the number of helpers makes a difference to a candidate's vote, but even if it does not, a larger campaign team is desirable for most candidates. This is because it can afford their campaign an air of legitimacy with the public, which in itself usually delivers more votes.

Personal computers

One of the most important features of a modern election-eering campaign is a personal computer, which saves candi-dates enormous amounts of time and money. Menial manual tasks, such as the compilation of canvassing lists and the writing of letters to voters, can now be done with computers both effortlessly and much more quickly than in the pre-computer era. In addition, leaflets, posters, and newsletters can now also all be produced relatively cheaply from the comfort of the candidate's home, thus helping to lessen the

TABLE 6.3 USE OF PERSONAL COMPUTERS PER CANDIDATE (%)

Party	Used computer expert	Computerised register	Monitor lists	Corres-pondence	Internet
Fianna Fáil	29	30	13	74	20
Fine Gael	26	31	17	75	18
Labour	37	44	15	69	33
Prog. Dems.	48	43	22	78	43
Green Party	30	37	24	76	40
Sinn Féin	61	58	59	74	13
Others	31	18	10	51	25

Source: 2004 local election candidate survey, question 19.

impact of the gulf in resources between candidates from parties of differing sizes. The communications revolution enables a candidate to run a modern campaign on their own without the need for a backroom team; the widespread availability of the internet means that candidates need not even leave their own bedroom to promote a campaign.

As table 6.3 indicates, approximately one-third of party candidates use a designated computer expert for their campaign and the same proportion use a computerised electoral register. Sinn Féin candidates report the highest usage of computers for their campaigns, with close to 60 per cent availing of a computer expert and a computerised register (which can be purchased for a nominal fee and can be of great assistance when compiling canvassing lists and sending out election literature), on both counts more than twice the proportion within Fianna Fáil and Fine Gael reporting usage of such resources. Sixty per cent of Sinn Féin candidates also use a computer to monitor the numbers of voters canvassed, four times the proportion of Fianna Fáil, Fine Gael and Labour candidates. It is only when it comes to using a computer to correspond with voters that the other party candidates match Sinn Féin's efforts (at rates of 75 per cent). The latter party's candidates, however, seem less reluctant to promote their campaign on the internet, with 13 per cent doing so, in contrast to 40 per cent of Green Party and Progressive Democrat candidates. With the widespread availability of personal computers, we might have expected candidates' use of this resource to be more common. Indeed, the emergence of the worldwide web was hailed as a democratising force because its relatively low costs (compared to media advertising) could help level the electoral playing field between candidates with diverging amounts of resources. However, it must be borne in mind that internet accessibility in Ireland lags behind the OECD average, which fosters candidates' hesitancy regarding the usefulness of cyber-canvassing, especially at local elections. In any case, the increasingly sophisticated nature of software technology means that candidates need professionals to set up and maintain their websites, with the consequence that the disparity between candidates is replicated in cyberspace.[8]

Electoral register

Any ambitious candidate needs to have an electoral register, which contains details of electors' names and addresses, to mount a successful campaign. Without it, they might canvass streets of unregistered voters, or be blissfully unaware that friends and neighbours who have promised to vote for them may be registered in a different electoral ward. Most candidates recognise this importance as 86 per cent of party candidates and 76 per cent of Independents use an electoral register (see table 6.4 below). Despite the high numbers professing to use an electoral register, just as with computers, it is an underutilised resource by candidates, as only 30 per cent of those running for a party use it to write personal letters, 67 per cent use it to monitor canvassing, and 53 per cent use it to draw up a list of potential supporters among the electorate. The main variation between the parties' candidates is that, once again, those running for Sinn Féin are the most active, and those from the Green Party the least active. Ninety-two per cent of Sinn Féin candidates use an electoral register and 54 per cent use it to send a letter to voters; the comparative figures for the Green Party are 63 per cent and 8 per cent, significantly lower proportions.

TABLE **6.4** USE OF ELECTORAL REGISTER PER CANDIDATE (%)

Party	Used register	Personal letter	Record of canvass	Estimate support
Fianna Fáil	91	33	70	48
Fine Gael	89	26	76	55
Labour	83	27	65	52
Prog. Dems.	88	38	65	65
Green Party	63	8	38	33
Sinn Féin	92	54	79	75
Others	75	12	46	38

Source: 2004 local election candidate survey, question 20.

Campaign activities performed

Having examined the resources available to candidates, this section analyses the type of campaign activities carried out. With the advent of electoral competition, a variety of tactics have been employed to engineer a successful campaign. Achille Lauro, the shipping magnate and Monarchist Party mayor of Naples in the 1950s, used to distribute one shoe to voters on the eve of the election and, if he was elected, they would be rewarded with the essential other shoe.[9] While most candidates cannot afford to distribute free footwear (besides the undoubted illegality of such a manoeuvre), there are other cheaper (and legal) tactics they can employ to maximise their vote.

Type of Campaign Activities

To determine what their campaign involved, candidates were asked to identify which of ten standard election activities they undertook (see table 6.5). These were: door-to-door canvassing, distributing election material on the streets, sending letters or postcards to voters, telephone canvassing, erecting posters, speaking on the radio, television appearances, press conferences, speaking at public meetings, and organising public rallies.

Door-to-door canvassing is by far the most popular election activity, carried out by 99 per cent of party candidates and over 95 per cent of Independents. Its prominence is an example of the continued strength of pre-modern electioneering in Ireland, which, according to one 2002 general election candidate, persists because 'where this is carried out effectively it is by far the best method of making direct contact with individual voters'.[10] This style of electioneering is used not only to canvass for a vote, but also to find out from voters what issues concern them. Well-prepared candidates are therefore usually armed with either a dictaphone or notebook to record these issues, which can then be tackled later in the constituency office. Some councillors perform this activity on a continuous basis, which explains why Irish politicians are sometimes seen as the equivalent of welfare officers or local brokers. Such is the importance placed on this activity, only four party candidates abstained from door-to-door canvassing, with all bar one of these failing to win a seat.

'Poster-wars' have been described as another feature of pre-modern campaigning,[11] and a conspicuous feature of the

Irish landscape during an election is the sheer volume of posters adorning every type of upright structure, be it telegraph pole, lamp post, or even tree. Party candidates are quite active on this front, with 86 per cent of them engaging in this activity. Sinn Féin are again the most active, as 96 per cent of its candidates put up posters, with Fianna Fáil (82 per cent), Fine Gael (87 per cent), and Labour (87 per cent) lagging narrowly behind. Independents are the least active, as 25 per cent of them did not put up any posters, perhaps reflecting the gulf in resources between them and party candidates. This could also be due to other factors, as one Independent, for example, refused to erect posters for both environmental reasons and because he believed that their oversaturation had a negative effect on voters. Indeed, on one particular occasion, namely the Balbriggan ward in north Dublin in 1991, candidates competed on their 'greenness' to the extent that no posters were put up in the area.[12] It was this environmental factor that motivated the Minister for the Environment, Heritage and Local Government in 2009 to contemplate banning election posters (and the plastic ties that often remain long after the contest). Despite the cost and labour associated with this activity, there was a considerable level of opposition to the minister's proposals from some quarters. Ciarán Lynch TD maintained that posters 'play a very, very positive role in the operation of elections' and Joanna Tuffy, also a Labour TD, said that 'it's pandering to people who treat democracy and elections like it's some kind of untidy intrusion on their lives […] if elections are there you put up posters […] and then you make sure people take them down'.[13]

While public meetings are no longer as popular as they were in the pre-television age, they can still often be an important medium for candidates to get their message across, and to show the public where their alignments lie on certain key issues. Any candidate worth her or his salt attends these meetings, since those present are usually regular voters, constituting a ready-made bundle of votes to a candidate who can champion their cause. Sinn Féin candidates are more likely to share this belief in the importance of such meetings: 58 per cent of them speak at public meetings, considerably more than the one-third of Fianna Fáil, Fine Gael or Independent candidates who do so.

TABLE 6.5 ELECTION ACTIVITIES UNDERTAKEN PER CANDIDATE (%)

Activity	Fianna Fáil	Fine Gael	Labour	Prog. Dems.	Sinn Féin	Green Party	Others
Door-to-door canvassing	99	99	100	100	96	100	95
Distributing leaflets	43	60	65	42	58	58	51
Sent letters	46	43	40	50	21	46	22
Telephone canvassing	24	27	8	31	8	7	13
Erected posters	82	87	85	92	83	96	76
Spoke on radio	60	70	69	77	58	58	53
Television appearance	0	9	10	8	17	8	7
Press conference	2	1	6	0	21	33	8
Spoke at public meeting	36	39	44	42	50	58	37
Organised public rally	8	4	10	0	17	11	10

Source: 2004 local election candidate survey, question 14.

Two activities which can cost considerable amounts of money, and therefore may be out of the reach of many candidates, are telephone canvassing and sending personal letters or postcards to voters. While 22 per cent of party candidates partake in the former, the vast majority of these comprise those from Fianna Fáil, Fine Gael and the now-defunct Progressive Democrats. Fewer than one in ten candidates from the other parties use a telephone as a medium to contact voters. Nearly twice as many party candidates (42 per cent) as Independents (23 per cent) post correspondence, which may reflect the custom of the former using prepaid Oireachtas envelopes obtained from party colleagues in their constituency, a perk of which Independents, given their solitary position, cannot avail. The Green Party is the only party falling significantly below this mean, with as few as one in five of its candidates sending letters to voters.

The usually extensive coverage of local elections by local radio stations (certainly in contrast to its relative absence in the national media) renders it a vitally important resource to candidates. Two-thirds of party candidates avail of this source, with little deviation from the mean across the parties. While fewer Independents speak on radio (52 per cent), it is important to state that these proportions are not necessarily accurate reflections of candidate activity. The ultimate decision regarding candidates' featuring on radio rests with the broadcasters. It is safe to presume that all candidates would have participated if they had the chance, but obviously the radio stations deemed that some of them were not worthy of coverage. This also applies to television appearances, and there being no regional television stations in Ireland, the opportunities for local election candidates are limited. Less than 7 per cent of candidates featured on television, ranging from no Fianna Fáil candidates to 17 per cent of those from the Sinn Féin ranks.

Walking the streets to meet and greet people and distribute election leaflets is a popular activity, undertaken by more than half of all candidates. While one would imagine that this is more prevalent in urban than rural areas, a preliminary analysis of candidates' backgrounds indicates that region makes little difference. Surprisingly, Fianna Fáil candidates (barely more than four out of ten) are less active on the streets than those from the other parties. Prior to the emergence of television, public rallies were a vital ingredient in a successful electioneering campaign. Candidates addressed large crowds in public places, debating the issues on which they stood. The development of communication technology, with 24-hour news channels and the worldwide web, has heralded the decline of this medium, and it is no surprise that only 9 per cent of candidates undertake this particular form of electioneering.

Election Literature: Posters and Leaflets

Perhaps the most obvious sign of electioneering is the posters candidates erect and the leaflets they distribute throughout their constituency. 'Leaflet' is a somewhat vague term, as it includes a wide array of election literature, ranging from constituency newspapers to flyers to glossy pamphlets detailing information about the candidate. With the widespread use and availability of personal computers, it is now relatively easy to produce a high-quality and professional leaflet without having to expend large sums on a professional designer and printer. The most time-consuming task involves distributing them, and candidates rely on a team of volunteers to drop these in letterboxes and hand them out at large gatherings of people. The average number of leaflets distributed per candidate is 10,500, with Progressive Democrats distributing the most (almost 20,000) and Independents (under 8,000) the fewest. Not surprisingly, there is a huge difference in the numbers distributed in urban and rural areas; the former are a considerably smaller geographical size, making it far easier for candidates to cover. Almost 16,000 leaflets are handed out by candidates in large town and city areas, more than twice as many as the approximately 7,000 leaflets distributed in rural areas. Table 6.6 also accounts for regional disparity by detailing the number of leaflets distributed per local electorate; the Green Party had the greatest coverage (84 per cent of the electorate) and Independents the lowest (57 per cent). With 1,963 candidates in the field, this amounts to an approximate total of 20 million leaflets distributed during the campaign. While this appears rather a large amount for local elections, where the size of the total electorate is around 3 million, with 11 candidates per LEA (of which there were 181 in 2004) with an average of 11,000 electors, this amounts to less than one leaflet per elector from each candidate. Indeed, when asked what proportion of the electorate to which they distributed leaflets, candidates put their best estimate at 75 per cent. Posters are a much more costly item of expenditure than leaflets, which the availability of a personal computer cannot help to lower, since a professional printer is usually required to produce them. Some candidates apply economising measures by recycling their posters from previous elections. Whether or not they make a difference, posters often provide an invaluable perception of a competitive presence in a local area. To this end, party candidates put up on average almost 200 posters each.

TABLE **6.6** POSTERS AND LEAFLETS DISTRIBUTED BY CANDIDATES

Party	Leaflets	Posters	Posters per 100 voters	Leaflets per 100 voters	% Electorate covered by leaflets
Fianna Fáil	11,071	197	1.1	65	73
Fine Gael	10,513	164	0.9	66	75
Labour	11,218	198	1.2	64	73
Prog. Dems.	19,917	230	1.2	79	81
Green Party	13,800	205	1.5	84	74
Sinn Féin	12,466	261	1.4	75	84
Others	8,183	151	1.0	57	70

Source: 2004 local election candidate survey, questions 15, 16 and 17.

We can provide a tentative analysis of the relationship between posters and votes using a correlation technique. This provides a coefficient in value between -1 and $+1$, where the closer to zero, the weaker the relationship. The correlation coefficient between posters and votes is a modest 0.28 (albeit statistically significant); this indicates a moderately positive relationship between the two variables. Figures 6.1 and 6.2 graph this relationship. The first figure indicates why the correlation is rather weak: a lower number of posters does have a positive effect on a candidate's vote, but this relationship plateaus out, peaking at around 500 posters. However, from this point on, erecting more posters seems to be a futile exercise, as it appears to be associated with fewer votes (indicated by the declining trend-line). This may occur where a candidate is too much in the spotlight, and voters get fed up of seeing her or his face splashed on posters all over their constituency. This phenomenon affected Royston Brady in the 2004 European Parliament elections, when his overexposure was widely reckoned to have been a contributory factor to his defeat. This 'Royston Brady effect' is lessened somewhat when we control for a few outlier cases that drag the trend-line in a downwards fashion. This is done using a mathematical technique that gives the logarithm equivalents for posters, the new relationship for which is shown in figure 6.2. This new graph indicates that the curvilinear effect was due to the presence of a few extreme cases (that is, some candidates winning few votes but putting up a lot of posters). Just as one swallow does not a summer make, so also such extremities cannot be used to define a relationship. Figure 6.2 therefore provides a more reliable estimate of the relationship between posters and votes. Posters have a positive effect, but the rate of this

FIGURE 6.1 EFFECT OF POSTERS ON VOTES

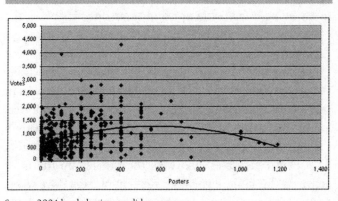

Source: 2004 local election candidate survey.

influence lessens the more posters put up (indicated by the decline in the gradient of the curve).

FIGURE 6.2 EFFECT OF POSTERS (LOGGED) ON VOTES

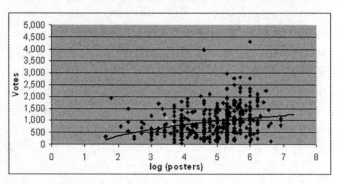

Source: 2004 local election candidate survey.

Polling Day

Candidates continue their campaign right up to polling day in the belief that even last-minute activities can be important in swinging a few extra votes in their direction. It is the culmination of candidates' campaigns, and if they cannot get their supporters out to vote, the weeks and months spent canvassing will have been wasted. Driving voters, especially the less mobile, to the polling station is still an important task, as is monitoring the turnout of potential supporters identified in the previous weeks' canvassing, especially if they are noticeable by their absence. Table 6.7 shows that Sinn Féin candidates, above all the others, are the most active on this front. Eighty-four per cent of them drive voters to the polling station, 42 per cent engage in last-minute leafleting, 33 per cent continue knocking on doors, 21 per cent of them canvass by telephone and 58 per cent of them drive around the constituency in a loudspeaker van. The only polling-day activity where Sinn Féin is not to the forefront is telephone canvassing, where it is outshone by Fine Gael candidates. Green Party candidates seem most averse to campaigning on polling day. Only 4 per cent of them drive voters to the polling station, none canvass by telephone and only 4 per cent drive a loudspeaker van. One activity we might expect most candidates to engage in is monitoring the electoral turnout at the polling stations, to check that their promised support shows up. While 71 per cent of Sinn Féin candidates do so, only one in two Fianna Fáil and Fine Gael candidates do so, a proportion that falls as low as 17 per cent for the Green Party.

TABLE **6.7** POLLING DAY ACTIVITIES CONDUCTED PER CANDIDATE

Party	Drive voters to polling station	Last-minute leafleting	Door-to-door canvass	Tele-phone canvass	Driving loudspeaker van	Monitoring turnout
Fianna Fáil	77	24	20	23	26	50
Fine Gael	69	33	22	34	17	57
Labour	46	25	13	6	17	33
Prog. Dems.	58	42	19	19	12	46
Green Party	4	33	8	0	4	17
Sinn Féin	84	42	33	21	58	71
Others	42	23	16	6	25	35

Source: 2004 local election candidate survey, question 21.

Campaign expenditure

One final measure of campaign activity is what candidates spend in their fight for a seat. In the absence of accurate details on the intensity and nature of campaigns, candidates' expenditure returns have often been used as a surrogate measure of campaigning. This study does not do so for two reasons. Firstly, we have a direct measure of campaign activities obtained from survey data; and secondly, while expenditure is a good measure of campaign intensity, it does not always tell the whole story. Just because a study of the previous local elections showed that money matters,[14] this does not mean that pouring funds into a campaign guarantees success. Expenditure matters simply because campaigning matters, and the latter usually costs money. Where candidates invest enough in the important campaign activities, ceteris paribus, this will lead to a greater vote return.

Table 6.8 below shows that the average amount spent per candidates was €3,473. However, because some parties run more than one candidate per constituency, this may not always portray a true picture of party expenditure. Therefore, even though most party candidates spent between €3,000

TABLE 6.8 CAMPAIGN EXPENDITURE

Party	N	Mean candidates per constituency	Mean expenditure (€)
Fianna Fáil	573	3.2	4,271
Fine Gael	479	2.7	3,514
Labour	211	1.2	3,456
Prog. Dems.	103	0.6	4,337
Green Party	111	0.6	1,866
Sinn Féin	148	0.8	3,077
Others	304	1.6	2,917

Source: Candidate expenditure returns supplied to author by individual city and county councils.

and €4,000 each, €13,000 was spent by Fianna Fáil candidates per constituency, in contrast to under €3,000 by Sinn Féin. While these could be the more accurate figures to use when assessing the differences in campaign expenditure, it is also valid to analyse candidates separately. This is because the decentralised and candidate-centred nature of local elections entails party candidates running their campaigns largely independently of party headquarters.

What makes a strong campaign?

We have seen that the intensity of campaigning per candidate varies according to the nature of activity. While only the Green candidates, for example, spent less than those from Sinn Féin, in most areas the latter was more active than all the other parties. Rather than stating each of these differences per activity, in this section a measure is devised that incorporates the six components of campaigning already discussed. Replicating the methodology of Denver and Hands,[15] this index is constructed using a statistical technique known as a principal components analysis. The aim of this is to establish whether there is a common underlying structure within a group of variables that links them together and to devise a single dimension that is a measure of this common structure. This dimension or index produces a scale of scores normalised around a mean of zero, where negative scores imply a candidate campaigned below the average level of activity and positive scores indicate a greater than average effort (see table 6.9). For example, Sinn Féin had the highest score of 1.17, while the Green Party and 'others' were below the mean level of campaigning (as indicated by their negative figures). If party candidates are ranked according to their level of campaign activity, Fianna Fáil trail in fourth place, behind both Fine Gael and the Progressive Democrats. Labour also does not fare too positively, as only the Green Party and 'others' are less active on the campaign trail than its candidates.

TABLE **6.9** CAMPAIGN SCORES FROM FACTOR ANALYSIS

Party	Campaign Index
Fianna Fáil	0.39
Fine Gael	0.47
Labour	0.19
Prog. Dems.	0.42
Green Party	−0.80
Sinn Féin	1.17
Others	−0.62

Source: 2004 candidate survey.

To gain an overview of the level of campaigning across the country, figure 6.3 details the performance of candidates in each city and county electoral area. Regions are shaded according to the mean score on the campaign index achieved by candidates within the constituency. Generally speaking, the darker the hue per region, the greater the intensity of campaign activity (for more detail see the colour-coded scale of intensity in figure 6.3). What is immediately obvious from the map is that campaigning is more intense in city areas, as Sligo, Dublin, Cork, Galway and Waterford all report higher than average levels of campaign intensity. The only exception is Limerick, where candidates are more active in the county than the city boroughs. Across rural areas, campaign activity is below the average, although there are a few notable exceptions, including Donegal, Clare, Tipperary, Carlow and Offaly. This urban–rural disparity does not necessarily mean

FIGURE 6.3 INTENSITY OF CAMPAIGNING PER CITY AND COUNTY ELECTORAL AREA

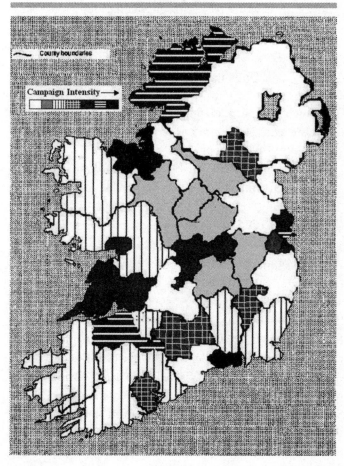

that candidates in the countryside are lazier than their city counterparts. Rather, it is a lot easier for urban candidates (despite the larger-sized electorates in their constituencies) to canvass their constituents, simply because of the greater population density of these regions. While these candidates' response might be that they have far more constituents to canvass, it is easier to campaign among more voters in a confined area than fewer voters in a more dispersed region.

Does campaigning matter?

Although some candidates may engage in campaigning for ritualistic purposes, for most the ultimate aim is to win more votes. With the percentage of candidates' first preference votes as the dependent variable (that is, the item we wish to explain) the influence of the six main components of campaigning is assessed by including them in an ordinary least-squares (OLS) multiple regression analysis. The aim of this technique is to assess the collective influence of a number of factors. It is necessary because if we isolate one factor, such as posters, what appears to be a significant relationship may be due to posters depending on something else. In addition to the different forms of campaigning, several other important aspects of an election are included, specifically candidates' status as an incumbent or challenger, and the size of the electorate in the constituency. The latter needs to be accounted for because one of the most important factors determining how many votes candidates win is the number of available voters. The results of this analysis are presented in table 6.10 below.

TABLE 6.10 OLS REGRESSION OF VOTE ON CAMPAIGN VARIABLES

Activity	Fianna Fáil	Fine Gael	GP, SF, PDs Lab	Indeps.	All Cands.
Preparation	0.20	0.18	0.09	0.21**	0.24***
Campaign team	0.11**	0.05	0.05	0.05*	0.06***
Leaflets	0.005	0.02	0.01	0.03*	0.02*
Posters	0.002	−0.0005	0.002	0.003*	0.002+
Resources	−0.10	0.42*	0.38	0.01	0.13
Canvas	−0.30	0.11	−0.006	0.003	−0.004
Polling day	−0.24	−0.08	−0.16	−0.06	−0.04
Incumbent	2.58**	4.12***	7.13***	4.69***	4.9***
Electorate	−0.0002***	−0.0002***	−0.0001*	−0.0001**	−0.0002***
Adj. R^2	0.21	0.40	0.35	0.30	0.35
N	89	86	109	170	467

* Indicates significance at 0.05 level; ** Indicates significance at 0.01 level;
*** Indicates significance at 0.001 level.
Note: the dependent variable is per cent of first preference votes.

To explain some of the figures in this table, adjusted r-squared refers to the proportion of the variance in the vote explained by the campaign variables, that is 35 per cent (or 0.35) of the variation in candidates' vote is due to their differing levels of campaign activity. N refers to the numbers in the sample, while the asterisks denote the statistical significance of the findings (one asterisk denotes a probability of one in twenty [0.05] of this result being due to chance; two asterisks a probability of one in one hundred [0.01]; and three asterisks a probability of one in one thousand [0.001]). Where there are no asterisks, the relationship described could be due to sheer randomness because a sample was used. The other figures denoted are regression coefficients, which indicate the change in the vote resulting from a unit increase in the respective campaign activity. For example, one extra poster brings a candidate an additional 0.002 per cent of the vote; so 1,000 posters should deliver 2 per cent extra votes. Similarly, councillors start the campaign with an advantage of 4.9 per cent more votes than challengers. While the 'all candidates' column indicates that preparation, campaign team, leaflets, posters, and incumbency all matter for candidates, this is in some ways due to the large number of Independents in the sample. When party affiliation (or lack of) is controlled for, these same campaign activities still retain their influence for Independents, but not for the other party candidates. Having more volunteers on a campaign team has a positive effect for Fianna Fáil, but interestingly, three activities have a negative effect for this party's candidates. As indicated by the negative coefficients, the more resources, canvassing and polling day activities carried out by Fianna Fáil candidates, the more votes they lose. In fact, polling day activities have a negative relationship with all candidates' votes. This does not necessarily mean that campaigning on the day of the election loses votes, but candidates' increased efforts are probably a reflection of their lack of activity over the previous months.

Looking at other candidates, it is difficult to indicate precisely how campaigning affects the vote of the minor parties, but this is probably because they were merged into one umbrella category to create a reasonable-sized sample for analysis. For Fine Gael candidates, every possible use that they squeezed out of computers and the electoral register brought them an extra half a percentage point of votes. For Independents, every additional 10 per cent of voters to whom they delivered a leaflet won them 0.3 per cent votes; 1,000 posters got them 3 per cent, while each additional level of preparation delivered 0.2 per cent of the vote. The findings that campaigning matters more for Independents is not surprising. This is because for most candidates the purpose of campaigns is to inform voters about their running, their issues, and so forth. Because Independents lack an identifiable party label and a central headquarters from which to draw resources, they are at a major disadvantage vis-à-vis party candidates. Campaigning is thus an essential activity for Independents to inform voters and to lessen the gap between them and established politicans. This hypothesis also holds for challengers, who face a difficult task to oust incumbents. In summary, these results indicate that campaigning is important for giving candidates a leg-up. For those who do not need this, the main purpose of campaigning is to ensure a converted voter turns out, but also because it is part of the ritualistic conflict of politics. An interesting side note is that since local elections are often a mid-term comment on the performance of the government, some candidates affiliated to governing parties may feel that an 'in-your-face' presence is not good for their electoral prospects. For example, reminding voters that one is the Fianna Fáil candidate might serve little good other than to reinforce the message in voters' minds that they must punish this party in the polls. In this respect, three campaign activities actually had a negative effect on the Fianna Fáil vote, that is, the harder its candidates campaigned, the more votes they lost.

Conclusion

Irish election campaigns have traditionally tended to buck the comparative models, as the focus was never solely on the national campaigns, but also on the contests within each electoral constituency, both between and within parties. Campaigning was very much a decentralised affair, with very little national co-ordination; all focus was on the individual constituency campaigns. While it can be said that general elections in Ireland have become modernised greatly since the 1970s – a trend marked by the increasing reliance of the large parties on focus group research, opinion polls and political spin – this has yet to permeate to local elections. As has been detailed here, pre-modern and modern campaigning are still very much an important part of electioneering, Irish-style. Knocking on doors with teams of volunteers, distributing leaflets in shopping centres, and speaking to after-church gatherings are *de rigueur* election conduct for all ambitious candidates. The high level of campaigning carried out by candidates re-affirms the adage that all politics is indeed local. This is especially so when we consider that it is difficult to gauge the precise electoral reward that campaign activities yield for candidates. In fact, the relatively weak influence of campaigns on the votes of established candidates would suggest that they are more rituals than vote-winning tactics. Campaigning at local elections is about something other than winning a seat: it is about providing a service to constituents. In spite of this finding, the reward for which may be more of intrinsic (i.e. a satisfaction stemming from helping someone out) than electoral value, it would be a brave candidate who rejects the ritual of local electioneering.

7

Local Election Behaviour, 1967–2004

U p to this point in the book, we have provided an analysis
of how local elections are conducted, why someone
would want to run for local office and an assessment of the
key components of a local campaign. However, is there
anything distinctive about local elections in Ireland that
warrants devoting a book to them? In this chapter we
undertake such an examination, in particular by focusing on
the patterns of voting behaviour, the nature of the parties and
candidates contesting the elections, and their use of the local
arena. This analysis is important because if we find that both
competition and behaviour at local elections differs from that
at general elections, it would cast doubt on the strength of
voters' partisan identities that are often so readily assumed.
On the other hand, if we find similar patterns at both levels,
we can conclude that local elections are merely a subset of
the national arena. Rather than analyse each election
piecemeal, in this chapter the key findings are summarised
under a number of headings. We begin with voter turnout.

1. Fewer people turn out to vote at local elections

Given the relative weakness of local government vis-à-vis its national counterpart, this is hardly a great surprise. As figure 7.1 indicates, average turnout at general elections is usually ten percentage points greater than at local elections. It is quite noticeable that the trend of turnout at the local level closely matches that at the national level. Just as turnout for Dáil elections steadily declined from 77 per cent in 1969 to 62 per cent in 2002 before suddenly increasing in 2007, so too turnout at the local level fell from 68 per cent in 1967 to 51 per cent in 1999 before surprisingly increasing in 2004 to 59 per cent. The similarity of this pattern is particularly marked when we consider that there has been a variety of other ballots held occasionally (albeit more frequently now)

FIGURE 7.1 TURNOUT AT LOCAL AND GENERAL ELECTIONS, 1967–2007

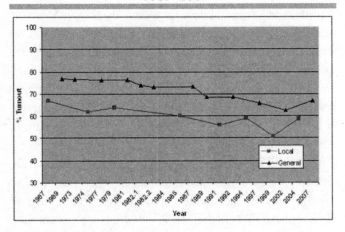

Source: Greene (2003), p. 101; www.environ.ie

in conjunction with local elections. European Parliament elections have been held on the same day in 1979, 1999 and 2004, as is the case again in 2009. Similarly, referenda have also coincided with local elections in both 1999 and 2004.

While we might assume that fewer people vote at local elections because they are less important than the national arena, voters are less discerning when it comes to the type of local election at which they vote. As table 7.1 below indicates, with the exception of Dublin, there is limited variation in turnout at county, borough and town council level, even though the latter has very little power. A simple premise to explain this is that, with the exception of 1994, elections across different levels are usually held on the same day. Only a very small minority choose to decline a vote for one arena when they have already turned out to cast another vote. That said, turnout did not dip dramatically when elections to only borough and town councils were held in 1994 (although they did coincide with European Parliament elections). The main source of variation is between county and city councils, with turnout anything from 5 to 10 per cent lower at the city level. This trend is not unusual to Ireland as turnout is usually higher in rural (our proxy for county councils) than in urban areas. Dublin City Council, in particular, experiences an even lower level of turnout, on average 15 per cent less than that for county councils. However, this is not an experience unique to local elections. Turnout at Dáil elections in Dublin city has always been lower than both its environs and rural areas, with the difference close to 15 per cent in 2007. This evidence supports the premise that local elections do not inspire any hugely different forms of behaviour from national elections (with the obvious exception of lower turnout).

TABLE 7.1 TURNOUT AT LOCAL ELECTIONS, 1967–2004

Local authority	1967	1974	1979	1985	1991	1994	1999	2004
City Councils (excl Dublin)	67	57	59	51	54	–	46	55
Dublin City Council	52	40	48	43	43	–	35	52
County Councils	72	68	67	63	58	–	53	60
Borough and Urban District Councils	69	65	64	62	–	59	54	56
Town Commissioners	73	70	70	66	–	56	52	58
Average	67	62	64	60	56	59	51	59

Note: Turnout in the Borough and Urban District Councils for 2004 refers to Borough Councils and those for Town Commissioners in 2004 refers to Town Councils.
Source: Greene (2003), p. 101; www.environ.ie

2. Fianna Fáil performance is weaker at local elections than at general elections

Since the 1985 local elections, when Fianna Fáil profited from a high level of dissatisfaction with the Fine Gael–Labour government, its average vote at local elections has been 33 per cent. In contrast, it has managed to win almost 42 per cent at Dáil elections over the same time period (see table 7.2 below). As Charlie McCreevy, then a backbench Fianna Fáil TD, put it in 1991, 'Fianna Fáil do badly in local elections as against general elections'.[1] A number of hypotheses could explain the party's under-performance at the local level, but perhaps the most relevant is its longevity in office. Across comparative political systems, governments traditionally fare poorly at mid-term second-order elections. The term second-order is used because such elections are secondary in importance to primary 'first-order' (i.e. general) elections. Since the formation of government is not at stake at these elections, voters often act in a more sincere fashion, picking the candidates they prefer; this is in contrast to the strategic incentives that motivate voters at Dáil elections to choose parties they would like to be in office. In addition, regardless of the sincerity or strategic nature of their decision, sometimes voters like to keep governments in check by punishing them at mid-term elections. The motivation to punish may also be exacerbated by the governing parties, who often manage the economy in such a way that unpopular measures are dealt with in the initial years of their term (i.e. in the run-up to local elections), before doling out the more popular policies prior to the more important general election. Because Fianna Fáil is in government far more often than the other parties (as has been the case during nine of the fourteen local elections it has contested), it tends to be the recipient of such negative sentiment from voters at local elections.

In the period detailed in table 7.2, Fianna Fáil's vote has rarely crept beyond 40 per cent, with 1985 a key exception (described, again by Charlie McCreevy, as 'an aberration'[2]), – and this at a time when the party was out of government. Fianna Fáil's inability to match its national electoral performance at the local level is something that is acknowledged by those within the organisation; the 'party of the nation' struggles to be the 'party of the locality'. Of course, it is also the case that Fianna Fáil faces far greater competition at local than at national elections; as a party of government, Fianna Fáil has few rivals, but as a local organisation, opposition abounds. Not only does this include the traditional opposition of Fine Gael and Labour, but also an eclectic collection of Independents, often from within the Fianna Fáil 'gene pool'. Indeed, whether out of foresight or a coincidence,

TABLE **7.2** FIRST PREFERENCE VOTE WON BY PARTIES AT LOCAL
AND GENERAL ELECTIONS, 1967–2007

Year	Fianna Fáil	Fine Gael	Labour	Prog. Dems.	Green Party	Sinn Féin	Workers' Party	Others
2007	41.6	27.3	10.1	2.7	4.7	6.9	0.1	6.5
2004	**31.8**	**27.6**	**11.4**	**3.9**	**3.9**	**8.1**	**0.2**	**13.1**
2002	41.5	22.5	10.8	4.0	3.8	6.5	0.2	10.7
1999	**38.9**	**28.1**	**10.7**	**2.9**	**2.5**	**3.5**	**0.5**	**12.9**
1997	39.3	27.9	10.4	4.7	2.8	2.6	0.4	11.9
1992	39.1	24.5	19.3	4.7	1.4	1.6	0.7	8.8
1991	**37.9**	**26.4**	**10.6**	**5.0**	**2.0**	**1.7**	**3.7**	**12.7**
1989	44.1	29.3	9.5	5.5	1.5	1.2	5.0	3.9
1987	44.1	27.1	6.4	11.8	0.4	1.9	3.8	4.5
1985	**45.5**	**29.8**	**7.7**	–	**0.6**	**3.3**	**3.0**	**10.1**
1982.2	45.2	39.2	9.4	–	–	–	3.1	3.2
1982.1	47.3	37.3	9.1	–	–	1.0	2.2	3.2
1981	45.3	36.5	9.9	–	–	–	1.7	6.6
1979	**39.2**	**34.9**	**11.8**	–	–	–	**2.3**	**11.8**
1977	50.6	30.5	11.6	–	–	–	1.6	7.3
1974	**40.1**	**33.7**	**12.8**	–	–	–	**1.5**	**11.9**
1973	46.2	35.1	13.7	–	–	–	1.2	5.0
1967	**40.2**	**32.5**	**14.8**	–	–	–	–	**12.5**

Source: Gallagher, 1989; Department of Environment and Local Government (1991, 2000, 2004).
Note: local election results are in bold font.

some within the party wanted to abolish local government. A government memo in 1933 said that 'governmental intervention and supervision is now feasible in respect of all national activities. The retention of local government bodies is, therefore, gradually becoming an expensive anachronism'.[3]

3. Independents perform better at local than general elections

Just as Fianna Fáil, the governing party, seems to suffer from voters acting more sincerely at local elections, Independents (including some minor groups) profit from this behaviour. While the average vote for Independents at general elections since the 1960s is less than 7 per cent, it has been almost double this figure (12 per cent) at local elections held in the same period. Because neither national issues nor government formation are to the fore at local elections, it affords an opportunity for local grievances to be aired. Consequently, groups and candidates mobilised over issues such as potholes, planning and the retention of services that include post offices and hospitals emerge to contest these elections. Because of the frequent election of hospital candidates in Roscommon, this has come to be known in some quarters as the 'Roscommon factor'.[4] This is still very much in evidence, as Independents won six of twenty-six council seats in Roscommon in 2004, with one candidate, John Kelly, winning more votes than the sum total of the three Fianna Fáil candidates in the Ballaghdereen constituency. There are a number of reasons why voters are more likely support such candidates at local elections. Given the relative weakness of local government, voters may feel they have little to lose by voting for a 'pothole' candidate at this level. In addition, while they may vote strategically for their preferred government at general elections, local elections may be viewed as an opportunity to indulge and vote for a localistic candidate they would normally be less inclined to support. This is particularly due to the candidate-centred nature of local elections, where party label is less important and personality is the key factor (this is particularly evident from a perusal of candidates' election literature, in which party affiliation is often downplayed, or in some cases, not mentioned at all). Given their lack of a party 'brand', this means that Independents are at less of a disadvantage vis-à-vis party candidates at local elections. Not only that, but Independents are more likely to emerge at local elections because they have a greater chance of winning a seat than at Dáil elections. The combination of multi-seat constituencies and the relatively low number of voters per constituency, means that an Independent could be elected in most cases with fewer than 1,000 votes. The small territorial size of local election constituencies also affords Independents a realistic opportunity to canvass all voters. On a comparative basis, there is often a strong element of non-partisanship to local elections to the extent that in some case parties are not allowed to field candidates (as is the case in many US states). Although parties are not banned from local elections in either the UK or France, in both these countries there are many districts (especially in rural areas) that have a tradition of electing Independent-dominated councils. While these non-partisan traditions have not permeated to the Irish case – despite Cumann na nGaedheal's aspirations in the 1920s – local elections are traditionally viewed as an arena where there is greater toleration and a greater demand for Independent representation. These beliefs are a partial factor in Independents' electoral strength at local level.

4. The national party system permeates to the local level

In some countries the parties competing at local elections differ quite significantly from those contesting national elections. We have already mentioned the tendency for non-partisanship in some systems, but there are also parties who focus solely on local elections. Examples in the UK include the Boston Bypass Independents and the Idle Toad Party, with the former managing to win an impressive twenty-five out of thirty-two seats to Boston Borough Council in Lincolnshire in 2007. There have also been examples of parties in Ireland that only contest local elections, including the Christian Principles Party (which fielded thirteen candidates in 1991, none of whom were successful) and Militant Labour (it had a town councillor elected in 1994). However, in contrast to their UK counterparts, none of these could be called localistic. These types of local parties are also few in number, and in any case, these two specific parties later contested Dáil elections under different names.

While the national parties in the UK and elsewhere afford their minor challengers some leeway in the local political game, in some cases by not even opposing them, this does not happen in Ireland. The Dáil parties prefer to maintain their dominance at all levels of governance. For these, local elections are inextricably linked to the national level. All parties use the local arena as a recruiting ground for future parliamentarians, which Fine Gael did in a successful manner at both the 1979 and 2004 elections. The new councillors elected in these years provided the launch pad for the party's gain of twenty Dáil seats at both succeeding general elections (in 1981 and 2007). This notion of the local level being a training ground is borne out by the evidence in tables 7.4 and 7.5 (see pp 158 and 160), where it is clear that most general election candidates had previously run at local elections (where permitted), and that before the ban on holding a dual mandate, the vast majority of TDs were also county or city councillors. There is therefore no sense of a clear distinction between politicians as councillors and as parliamentarians. Most of the former aspire to a career as the latter, while most of the latter fear a rival emerging from the former. This explains why TDs traditionally retained their council seat to keep a watchful eye on local competition. The parties also use local elections to ensure that their organisation is in active mode for the next general election and to make direct contact with the electorate during the interim period.[5] Fianna Fáil, for example, used the local elections in the early years of its existence to build up the organisation, to get its members involved in political campaigns and to strengthen the loyalty of its supporters.[6] Similarly, Fianna Fáil's electoral losses in 2004 resulted in an internal investigation into the party's organisational structure, without which it is likely that the party would not have been re-elected against the odds in 2007.

Other factors giving local elections a national feel include the method of electing the Seanad, the timing of local elections and the campaign strategies of the opposition parties. Because the forty-three panel senators are picked by an electorate dominated by councillors, the national parties have an incentive to win as many local seats as possible. Since the local elections are always held between general elections, it affords them a mid-term air, ensuring that local elections will involve an element of a half-time assessment of the government's performance. Finally, for this reason, the opposition parties often try to run their local election campaigns on national issues, which, depending on circumstances, the governing parties try to avoid. For the 1985 local elections, for example, Fine Gael (in government at the time) did not issue a national manifesto because the party did not see it as a national election. Fine Gael headquarters spent only a few thousand pounds on the campaign, as the party claimed it was entirely focused on its local candidates promoting local issues.[7] Fianna Fáil, in contrast, focused its campaign on the government's performance both nationally and internationally, specifically the state of the economy and Anglo-Irish relations. The party's aim was to capture as large a national vote as possible and to undermine the credibility of the government; to this extent, the Fianna Fáil leader Charles Haughey ordered all TDs, with the exception of himself and deputy leader Brian Lenihan, to put their names forward for selection conventions.[8] This can be seen as a form of domino theory, whereby gains at one level will have knock-on effects at another level. Most parties subscribe to this thesis, believing that success at local elections will reap dividends at the next Dáil elections. The evidence does not always support this theory, however, as record gains made by both Sinn Féin and Labour in 2004 did not translate into increased success at the 2007 general election. Similarly, Fianna Fáil's losses in 2004 did not prevent the party from increasing its national vote in 2007. This might lead to the suggestion that there are separate forms of behaviour at both local and general elections, something that is explored in the next section.

5. Electoral behaviour at local v. general elections

In 1999 Noel Whelan observed one of Fine Gael's European candidates, Avril Doyle, picking up large volumes of votes from polling districts in Wexford where Fianna Fáil candidates were concurrently dominant in the count for the local elections.[9] While this may suggest evidence of different sets of electoral behaviour at the local and European level, to what extent does this behaviour differ between the local and Dáil level? We have already seen that at local elections support for Fianna Fáil declines, while it increases for Independents. However, these national aggregates are not reliable measures for determining patterns of support. For example, a party may receive a similar vote at national and local elections, but this may mask large disparities at the constituency level. To test the similarity in electoral behaviour, the method used here is to compare a party's vote per constituency at local election to its vote in the same constituencies at general elections. This method replicates that used by Gallagher for elections between 1967 and

1989,[10] so this section focuses on elections held in the period since, i.e. 1991 to 2007. The smallest electoral unit for which data is available from general elections is the constituency level. Owing to the division of counties and difficulties in comparing Dublin constituencies, there are twenty-five manageable units that can be compared between Dáil and council elections (for further details see the notes below table 7.3). The method of analysis is a simple correlation. This produces a coefficient on a scale of −1 to +1 where −1 implies a perfect negative relationship and +1 a perfect positive relationship. The closer the coefficient is to 0, the weaker the relationship. A perfect relationship means that we can precisely predict the vote at one level if we know the vote at the other level.

By comparing the correlation coefficients across local and national elections we can determine if there are different patterns of electoral behaviour. If the higher coefficients are for elections of the same variety, this would lend support to this hypothesis. If, on the other hand, the higher coefficients are for proximate elections this would indicate that voters treat local and general elections as one and the same type. Details of the correlation coefficients for Fianna Fáil, Fine Gael and Labour at the 1991, 1999 and 2004 locals and the 1992, 1997, 2002 and 2007 general elections are provided in table 7.3 below. If we compare Fianna Fáil's coefficients, its local election vote in 2004 is highly correlated with its local vote in 1999 (0.88) and 1991 (0.86), yet weakly correlated with its national vote in 2002 (0.30) and 1997 (0.44). Similarly the party's general election vote in 2007 is more than moderately correlated with its 2002 performance

(0.63) (although not 1997), but very weakly with its local vote in 2004 (0.09), 1999 (0.03) and 1991 (-0.05). In fact, the relationship between Fianna Fáil's vote at the 2007 general election and its vote at the last three local elections is almost non-existent. What exactly does this mean? As has already been detailed, the large vote Fianna Fáil attracts at general elections is not retained at local elections. This would suggest that those voting for Fianna Fáil at general elections desert the party at the local level, but return at the next general election (as is indicated by the relatively strong correlation between the Fianna Fáil vote in 2002 and 2007). Perhaps, however, the assumption that Fianna Fáil's vote at national elections is its normal level is misplaced.[11] Instead it could be the case that the party's true level of support is what it receives at local elections, and that Fianna Fáil's vote rises at national elections when voters switch to it as the 'natural' party of government. The high correlations between Fianna Fáil's vote at the 1991, 1999 and 2004 local elections add extra weight to this hypothesis: even when the party's vote plummeted in 2004, it was still strongly related to the vote it had received five and thirteen years previously. While it certainly seems that the pattern of support for Fianna Fáil at local elections is of a different type from the vote it attracts at general elections, in the absence of more data, it is difficult to tell which is the party's true level of support.

Electoral behaviour towards both Fine Gael and Labour does not provide evidence of two distinct types. Fine Gael's vote in 2007 bore a strong level of similarity with its vote at the 2004 locals (0.84), the 2002 nationals (0.83), the 1999 locals (0.81) and the 1997 nationals (0.84). Although there

TABLE **7.3** CORRELATION OF LOCAL AND DÁIL ELECTORAL
BEHAVIOUR, **1991–2007**

Fianna Fáil

Year	2007	2004	2002	1999	1997	1992
2004	0.09					
2002	0.63	0.30				
1999	0.03	0.88	0.37			
1997	0.29	0.44	0.64	0.62		
1992	-0.16	0.61	0.28	0.66	0.49	
1991	-0.05	0.86	0.23	0.86	0.55	0.63

Fine Gael

Year	2007	2004	2002	1999	1997	1992
2004	0.84					
2002	0.83	0.82				
1999	0.81	0.93	0.79			
1997	0.84	0.79	0.82	0.77		
1992	0.62	0.60	0.67	0.65	0.64	
1991	0.56	0.80	0.62	0.85	0.51	0.56

Labour

Year	2007	2004	2002	1999	1997	1992
2004	0.89					
2002	0.87	0.85				
1999	0.91	0.96	0.86			
1997	0.59	0.49	0.64	0.63		
1992	0.75	0.78	0.69	0.83	0.72	
1991	0.71	0.73	0.71	0.83	0.67	0.82

Notes: 1992, 1997, 2002 and 2007 were general elections; 1991, 1999 and 2004 refer to local elections.

The twenty-six geographical units of analysis (i.e. predominantly counties) for the correlational analysis in this table are: Carlow-Kilkenny, Cavan-Monaghan, Clare, Cork city, Cork county, Donegal, Fingal, South Dublin, Dublin city, Dún Laoghaire–Rathdown, Galway, Kerry, Kildare, Laois–Offaly, Limerick, Longford–Roscommon, Louth, Mayo, Meath, Sligo–Leitrim, North Tipperary, South Tipperary, Waterford, Westmeath, Wexford, Wicklow.

are some differences in the correlations when comparing the party's vote at other elections, these are quite small, certainly not large enough to reject the hypothesis that local electoral behaviour for Fine Gael is any different from the pattern of support for the party at Dáil elections. Pretty much the same conclusion is reached from an analysis of Labour's voting figures. This evidence is not in line with the central premise from the Fianna Fáil data, i.e. that a party attracts a different geographical base of support at local than at general elections. We cannot therefore conclude that behaviour at local elections is a separate and independent form to that which takes place at general elections; rather, it is simply a different variant.

One alternative method of comparing electoral behaviour at local and Dáil level is to examine the transfer patterns between candidates. As already mentioned, party is less important at local elections and non-partisanship is more prevalent, so we can hypothesise that this should imply that the levels of internal transfer solidarity between party candidates is lower at local than general elections. Although this data is available for only a few local elections, and although it does not discount cases where there was not another same-party candidate available to receive transfers, we can compare like with like using data compiled by Donnelly (1992, 1999). As predicted, at local elections there is more cross-party voting than takes place at general elections. For example, while 70 per cent of Fianna Fáil votes transferred to other Fianna Fáil candidates (itself a record low for the party) in the 1992 general election, less than 55 per cent of Fianna Fáil votes stayed within the party fold in

1991, with 18 per cent transferring to Fine Gael candidates. Likewise, 65 per cent of Fine Gael votes transferred to other Fine Gael candidates in 1992, but at the previous year's local elections less than 45 per cent did, while 14 per cent transferred to Fianna Fáil. Comparing the transfer patterns at the 1997 general and 1999 local election, similar results are found. While Fianna Fáil had a transfer rate of 55 per cent within the party in 1997, this fell to 47 per cent two years later. Across the same two elections, Fine Gael's transfer solidarity declined from 52 to 40 per cent.[12] Similar figures for the other parties are not reliable because there are relatively few cases for the other parties where they ran more than one candidate thus limiting the options for a robust analysis. What the results indicate are that voters are less committed to particular parties at local elections and that they are more likely to switch their lower preferences across parties. A possible influence on transfer destination at the local level could be geography, whereby voters cast their preferences according to their proximity to candidates. While casual observation of tally data lends some credence to this theory, in the absence of more data from local elections, it is difficult to verify this hypothesis.

6. Local government is a springboard for national office

Most politicians run for local office as a prelude to national politics. As table 7.4 details, before 2003 approximately two-thirds of general election candidates for both Fianna Fáil and

Fine Gael had run at the previous local elections (where almost all of them had been elected as a councillor). While this number fell dramatically in 2007 as a result of the ban on holding a dual mandate, this does not mean that fewer electoral virgins are running for office. Excluding the incumbent TDs and senators who ran in 2007, of the remaining 205 party candidates, 103 were councillors, 47 had already unsuccessfully contested public elections, while only 55 (i.e. one in four) had not run for office before.[13]

TABLE 7.4 PROPORTION OF GENERAL ELECTION CANDIDATES CONTESTING PRECEDING LOCAL ELECTIONS (%)

Year	Fianna Fáil	Fine Gael	Labour	Others
2007	20	42	41	41
2002	66	76	74	47
1992	61	84	88	45
1987	69	64	49	38
1981	55	59	56	41
1977	65	69	64	41

Note: both this table and table 7.5 only compare adjacent general and local elections. For example, the 1987 Dáil election is compared to the 1985 local election, while the 1989 Dáil election is not included in this comparison.
Source: for this and Table 7.5, Department of the Enviroment (1974, 1979, 1985, 1991, 1999, 2004), *Nealon's Guides* to the various general elections.

Not only is local office a springboard to launch national careers, but, in keeping with the water-based metaphor, it has also been used as a lighthouse by TDs to keep a watchful eye on their constituencies. The aims of this strategy are both to satisfy the demands of local voters and to monitor potential electoral competition. To this extent, before the aforementioned ban on the dual mandate, the vast majority of TDs were also councillors (which was the main rationale for the ban). Details of the respective figures per party are provided in table 7.5 below. This lists the proportion of candidates elected at a Dáil election who had also been elected at the preceding local elections. Again, the dual mandate had a dramatic effect on these figures, because the only councillors contesting the 2007 Dáil elections were non-TDs. Prior to 2003, most TDs had been elected at the preceding set of local elections, rising to as high as 90 per cent for Fine Gael in 2002 and 94 per cent for Labour in 1992. The figures are slightly lower for Fianna Fáil because of its near-permanent presence in government; many of its ministers did not (and since 1991, could not) contest council elections. These figures therefore underestimate the value of local government as a stepping stone to national politics, because if we consider the proportion of TDs who were councillors before they were elected to the Dáil (i.e. not just at the last election), the figures are far higher. In 2007, for example, 77 per cent of TDs had first belonged to a local authority; the respective figures in 2002, 1997, 1992 and 1989 are 75 per cent, 74 per cent, 74 per cent and 71 per cent.[14] Prior to the ban on the dual mandate, it was quite obvious that the national system had permeated or even invaded the local level. The end of dual office-holding therefore has the potential to exert a major effect on the local political scene. There is now an increased level of competition at local elections, and indeed this is one of the reasons for Fianna Fáil's poor electoral performance in 2004. The party's big vote-getters, most of whom were also TDs, could not run for local office, and their personal support did not necessarily transfer to those Fianna Fáil candidates who ran in their place. However, for most of the reasons discussed in the previous section, the dual-mandate ban is unlikely to alter radically the form of local representation. The only change to date is that there are now more councillors who aspire to national office, which is likely to create greater competition at Dáil elections. It is, therefore, the national level that benefits from such changes, with the local level still remaining an inferior subset.

TABLE **7.5** PROPORTION OF SUCCESSFUL DÁIL CANDIDATES COMPRISING COUNCILLORS (%)

Year	Fianna Fáil	Fine Gael	Labour	Others
2007	12	24	10	6
2002	67	90	85	79
1992	53	76	94	67
1987	80	49	67	59
1981	54	68	86	50
1977	67	66	85	50

This denotes the proportion of TDs who were elected at preceding council elections in 2004.

Conclusion

This chapter has analysed a number of features of voting behaviour and party competition at local elections. It has been shown that the main differences in behaviour at local and national elections are that fewer people vote, fewer support Fianna Fáil, and more support Independent candidates. It has also been shown that the same parties that shape competition in the Dáil control local politics and that they often treat local elections as a mere subset of the national level. This is particularly the case with the manner in which local government is viewed as a breeding ground for potential Dáil candidates. While it has been found that local elections are not independent of Dáil elections, for either parties or voters, it is without doubt that the most significant force shaping local politics is the parties. If they afforded local government more power or even abstained entirely from this level, it would result in a very different political system. This aspiration was expressed in some quarters and an example of such sentiment was voiced in an editorial from *The Irish Times* in the run-up to the scheduled November 1923 locals (which were ultimately postponed):

> There seems to be a grave danger that the forthcoming elections will resolve themselves into another struggle between 'Free Staters' and 'Republicans'. We hope sincerely that this peril will be averted. Local elections ought to have no connection of any kind with 'high politics': the time for that sort of thing is over-past. The local boards in the Free State exist, not for the discussion of political problems, but for the efficient administration of boroughs and urban districts [...]. We hope earnestly that the Free State Government will not encourage the Cumann na nGaedheal to contest the local elections as a political party. The people everywhere are sick and tired of the political issue, and they want men at the head of their local affairs who will not waste time in sterile

discussions about prisoners or in passing resolutions of sympathy with this or that political party.[15]

Of course, parties did contest local elections, and while it was (and is) well within their democratic right to do so, one can only imagine the different type of system that would have evolved had local government adopted a non-partisan form. Regardless of the merits of the party politicisation of local elections, it is difficult to believe that this alternative evolution would have resulted in local government being seen as any less relevant among voters than is already the case.

Epilogue

What has been learned from this guide to Irish local elections? To begin with, as a classic form of second-order local elections, they are most definitely secondary in importance to general elections. Since local government has remained comparatively weak in the modern history of the Irish state, local elections have often been treated with scorn or derision by the political parties. Local elections have been used for blatant political purposes, postponed either to prevent the government getting a hammering at the polls, for example, or to avoid giving the opposition an opportunity to mobilise for a general election. There was little doubt that the latter was the intention of the Fianna Fáil–Labour coalition government when in 1994 it postponed the 1996 set of county and borough elections until 1998, the year after the next expected Dáil election. In this way, a potential new breed of councillors for the opposition parties would not have an impact at the national level until at least the following decade.[1]

While the constitutional recognition of local government and the fixing of election dates that has since taken place promised to improve the position of local government, in reality little has changed. Local government remains very much subservient to the national level. Those seeking genuine reform hoped that the ban on the dual mandate would end this – no longer would local councils be controlled by national parliamentarians whose interests were firmly focused on the centralised base of authority. In this way, the ban has the potential to provide daylight between local and national government, resulting in the election of genuine local councillors, as opposed to TDs looking to protect their bailiwick. At this early stage it is difficult to determine the effect of the dual mandate ban. Certainly, it had an impact in constituencies where parties were usually reliant on their TDs to deliver a vote at local elections. The ban is therefore more likely to affect the strategies of parties rather than radically reform local government. Parties will now have to recruit a greater number of capable candidates and will not be able to approach the local elections in a complacent manner, lest they suffer the fate that befell Fianna Fáil in 2004. This means that, because the gateways to local office are no longer guarded by TDs, there are now more opportunities for ordinary citizens to enter the political arena. This is no bad thing because getting more people involved in the political process can only improve the quality of the end product.

When we consider the function of local elections, while some might argue that the Seanad is traditionally a retirement home for politicians, local councils are very much a nursery. Parties use the latter as an arena to propagate new generations of politicians and to test the latter's mettle for a potential Dáil career. There are many examples of candidates selected at the local level, who may have promised much, but who lack either the will or ability to cut it as a full-time politician. It could also be argued that this filtering role or weeding-out process ultimately improves the quality of those elected to the Dáil. Competition, whether in the business sector or in politics, should improve the quality of the products on offer; after all, anyone not cut out for the contest will be tossed to the scrapheap in favour of a better rival. However, although this indicates the positive role played by local elections in the political process, if this is their sole purpose we have to question the utility of these elections. It is perhaps unfair to blame the parties or even the candidates for using local elections as a stepping stone to national office. After all, we want ambitious politicians as our elected representatives; if someone proves their worth at the local level, it is only natural that they should aspire for higher office. Would it really be desirable to have in place a group of politicians happy to remain at just the local level – what would this reveal about their abilities or even their foresight? Perhaps such councillors remain there because of a personal realisation of their limitations; surely it would be better to have in office individuals who believe they are capable of greater things and who act accordingly? On the other hand, it could be argued that the treatment of local government as an interim level undermines its relevance. Seen as a form of purgatory to be endured before passing through the pearly gates of Leinster House, this can result in a complacent attitude to local government that ensures councillors do whatever it takes to secure the party nomination for the next Dáil elections. An interesting area for future research to test the merits of these arguments would be to compare the activities of career local councillors and those who have moved onto the next level. If we found that those in local government for life achieved more for the local authority than those only resting there on the way to the Dáil, it would lend strong evidence to the calls for a complete separation of local and national government.

One area that we did not focus on was the issues that are likely to arise during a local campaign. The then Minister for the Environment, Pádraig Flynn, demonstrated an understanding of the essence of local elections when, shortly before the 1991 set, he announced that all potholes would be fixed within weeks. In the survey of local election candidates from 2004, on which a lot of data in this book were based, we sought to determine to what extent campaigns were mobilised on constituency-specific issues. To this end, candidates were asked to state the three most important issues of their campaign. A summary of the responses is detailed in table 8.1 below, where the figures denote the proportion within each party who cited the specific issue (listed in the rows). For example, planning was an important issue for 15 per cent of Fianna Fáil candidates, but for 23 per cent of Labour candidates. The health services were an important issue for 50 per cent of Sinn Féin candidates, but only 8 per cent of Green Party candidates. Looking at specific party patterns, Fianna Fáil candidates cited local (that is, specific to their respective constituency), health, traffic and housing issues. For Fine Gael it was health, housing, local issues, traffic, crime and housing. For Labour it was health, housing, local issues, traffic, crime and planning. Not surprisingly, economic issues were most important for Progressive Democrat candidates and traffic and planning for the Greens. Health and housing were the most important issues for Sinn Féin, while for 'others' it was local issues (reflecting the localistic bent of Independents), health and housing. While it is not altogether unexpected that the smaller parties exhibit differences in their focus because of their niche-driven nature, it is interesting to note the relative similarities between the two main parties of the Irish political system, Fianna Fáil and Fine Gael. We might have expected that Fine Gael, having not won a general election since 1982, might cite different issues from its Fianna Fáil counterparts, in power at national level almost continuously since 1987. However, Fine Gael candidates were only slightly more likely to cite health and crime as important issues, while the differences between the candidates on planning, the economy, education,

TABLE **8.1** ISSUES CITED BY CANDIDATES (%)

Issue	Fianna Fáil	Fine Gael	Labour	Prog. Dems.	Sinn Féin	Green Party	Others
Planning	15	12	23	27	33	4	16
Health	30	41	38	31	8	50	26
Local	39	27	25	35	21	29	32
Economy	9	6	6	15	8	0	5
Education	11	10	8	4	4	4	3
Housing	24	31	31	12	21	50	20
Crime	10	20	23	8	4	25	18
Traffic	28	27	25	27	50	4	16
No. of respondents	96	94	48	26	24	24	193

Note: the figures in each cell denote the proportion of candidates within each party for whom the respective issue was a strong feature of their campaign.
Source: 2004 local election candidate survey, question 2.

housing and traffic were not statistically significant. These similarities provide further confirmation of Weeks' claim (2009) that Fianna Fáil and Fine Gael, in terms of their policy positions, are comparable to Tweedledum and Tweedledee.[2]

While many of these issues cropped up again during the 2009 campaign, in many respects they paled in significance to the problems besetting the national economy, which is in marked deterioration compared to 2004. The opposition parties focused much of their campaign on the government's management of this issue, and to this extent, local elections are a case of *plus ça change, plus c'est la même chose*. The more things change, the more they remain the same, as once again local elections act as a mid-term assessment of the government's performance.

In conclusion, it has been shown that local elections can act as a forewarning for parties of what is to come. Many previous sets of local elections sowed the seeds of either future gains or losses at the Dáil level. For example, the 1979 locals marked the beginning of the end for Jack Lynch, and the gains made by Fine Gael set the foundation for the national electoral successes it achieved in the early 1980s. Likewise, Labour's winning an extra thirty-one council seats in 1991 continued a positive trend begun with Mary Robinson's election to the presidency, ultimately culminating in the 1992 'Spring Tide'. In light of these examples, 2004 was a somewhat unusual election. Fianna Fáil had record losses, barely winning more seats than Fine Gael, while both Labour and Sinn Féin strengthened their representation considerably. And yet at the Dáil elections three years later it was Fianna Fáil that was re-elected, winning 50 per cent more seats than Fine Gael; in addition, neither Labour nor Sinn Féin reaped the rewards that might have been expected following their respective local election performances. While the ban on the dual mandate was a factor in this deviant trend, these results indicate that a pattern moulded by local elections is not necessarily set into a concrete form.

What do these examples teach parties about local elections? Winning more seats and votes than at previous ballots is not necessarily the key benefit they can extract from local elections. Rather, producing electable candidates who will stand a good chance of winning a future Dáil seat is arguably more important for some parties. Of course, attracting such individuals is proving ever more difficult for parties. It was shown in chapter 5 that candidates are more likely to run when there is a tangible benefit accruing from their winning a seat, and to this end, one of the key incentives offered by parties is a potential nomination for a Dáil election. Not everyone, however, can secure such a nomination, which results in a lot of disappointed councillors. This goes some way to explaining the considerable number of local office-holders in particular areas to have resigned from councils in recent years. Dublin City Council is a prime example, where eleven councillors resigned from the 52-seat body between 2006 and 2008. While some may criticise the parties for not making local office more attractive as a position in its own right, until there is serious reform of local government, the type of carrot that can be offered by parties to candidates will remain a limited variety.

If electable candidates are recruited by the parties, getting them elected is the key activity. No matter how capable the individual, they are unlikely ever to make it as a politician if they fail to win a seat at the local level. As detailed in chapter 5, most TDs and government ministers first cut their political teeth in the local arena. It was therefore outlined in chapter 6 what the key aspects of a campaign are for candidates and what activities matter. The key finding is that campaigning is far more important for non-office holders as it helps to establish their presence in the field. For those already a councillor, campaigning is less important, and for those affiliated to a party in government at the national level, some campaigning can have a negative effect.

This book has provided an introduction to local elections in Ireland. The record of party and Independent candidates across generations has been outlined (see Appendix 1 for more specific details) as have been the various legislative acts guiding their behaviour. The latter half of the book focused on what candidates themselves thought of local elections, as we detailed why they stand and what they do during their campaigns. This book should therefore serve as a useful guide to those considering running for local office, those who have already done so and the general reader interested in local government, politics, or simply the workings of the system within which they reside. Whoever the reader, it should be obvious throughout the book of the significance of localism in the Irish political system. Somewhat ironic considering the centralised nature of government in Ireland, all politics is indeed local.

APPENDIX 1

Electoral performance at local elections
1974–2004
by Will Whitmore and Travis Johnson

TABLE A.1 NUMBER OF SEATS WON, AND CANDIDATES, BY PARTY,
1974 LOCAL ELECTIONS

County	Total	Fianna Fáil	Fine Gael	Labour	Sinn Féin	Others
Carlow	21–45	9–18	7–16	3–9	0–0	2–2
Cavan	25–52	12–20	10–18	0–3	0–0	3–11
Clare	31–63	19–8	7–17	2–8	0–1	3–9
Cork	46–84	20–30	17–30	6–17	1–1	2–6
Donegal	28–61	10–20	11–18	0–1	1–2	6–20
Dublin	25–80	9–22	9–21	5–18	0–2	2–17
Galway	31–66	16–25	9–23	1–5	0–2	5–11
Kerry	26–57	13–19	7–14	3–7	1–2	2–15
Kildare	21–55	10–20	7–19	3–12	0–2	1–2
Kilkenny	26–67	12–24	11–22	2–14	1–2	0–5
Laoighis	25–50	11–22	12–21	2–4	0–0	0–3
Leitrim	22–34	8–13	12–13	0–1	0–0	2–7
Limerick	27–47	14–22	11–17	2–4	0–0	0–4
Longford	21–40	8–15	8–15	0–2	0–0	5–8
Louth	26–69	11–23	10–22	1–8	1–3	3–13
Mayo	31–59	15–23	13–24	0–2	0–0	3–10
Meath	29–69	14–24	8–23	5–17	0–0	2–5
Monaghan	20–45	7–17	8–13	0–0	0–4	5–11
Offaly	21–47	9–14	8–17	3–9	0–0	1–7
Roscommon	26–50	11–19	12–19	0–2	0–1	3–9
Sligo	24–51	10–16	11–21	1–6	0–1	2–7
Tipperary NR	21–40	9–16	6–11	3–5	0–0	3–8
Tipperary SR	26–52	11–19	10–17	4–10	0–0	1–6
Waterford	23–53	12–19	7–18	2–7	0–2	2–7
Westmeath	23–55	11–21	6–19	2–7	0–0	4–8
Wexford	21–47	9–15	6–15	4–12	0–1	2–4
Wicklow	21–65	9–20	6–15	4–17	0–9	2–4
Total	687–1575	309–544	249–498	58–207	5–35	66–291

COUNTY BOROUGH

County	Total	Fianna Fáil	Fine Gael	Labour	Sinn Féin	Others
Cork	31–84	16–28	11–21	2–22	0–8	2–5
Dublin	45–135	15–36	13–31	10–29	0–4	7–35
Limerick	17–51	5–15	5–13	5–12	0–0	2–11
Waterford	15–36	6–10	3–8	2–6	1–3	3–9
Total	108–306	42–89	32–73	19–69	1–15	14–60
Total County & County Borough	795–1881	351–633	281–571	77–276	6–50	80–351

Note: In this and tables a.3, a.5, a.7, a.9 and a.11 the first figure in each column refers to the number of councillors elected and the second figure the number of candidates.[1]

TABLE A.2 TURNOUT AND PARTY PREFERENCE BY COUNTY, 1974 LOCAL ELECTIONS (%)

County	Voter Turnout	Fianna Fáil	Fine Gael	Labour	Sinn Féin	Aontacht Éireann	Others
Carlow	65	37.0	37.2	20.5	–	–	5.3
Cavan	75	39.1	39.0	2.1	–	1.3	18.5
Clare	71	54.1	25.3	7.5	0.4	–	12.7
Cork	70	41.6	37.2	15.2	1.9	–	4.1
Donegal	74	36.4	32.3	0.4	3.9	–	27.0
Dublin	48	30.7	34.6	23.2	0.6	1	9.9
Galway	66	49.3	31.5	5.6	0.8	–	12.8
Kerry	75	43.3	28.2	11.9	2.5	–	14.1
Kildare	59	45.7	30.2	20.2	1.5	–	2.4
Kilkenny	72	42.6	36.7	14.1	2.8	–	3.8
Laoighis	73	46.6	43.5	8.2	–	–	1.7
Leitrim	81	36.4	47.8	1.6	–	–	14.2
Limerick	74	53.5	36.4	7.1	–	–	3.0
Longford	78	38.6	40.9	1.5	–	0.6	18.4
Louth	68	38.6	34.0	8.4	3.1	–	15.9
Mayo	71	43.7	45.4	1.4	–	–	9.5
Meath	66	44.7	27.6	22.5	–	–	5.2
Monaghan	79	34.9	40.4	–	2.5	–	22.2
Offaly	70	41.1	36.2	12.7	–	2.7	7.3
Roscommon	76	39.3	43.3	1.6	1.7	–	14.1
Sligo	76	40.5	46.6	4.5	0.6	–	7.8
Tipperary NR	77	39.4	28.2	16.3	–	–	16.1
Tipperary SR	77	40.5	34.1	18.2	–	–	7.2
Waterford	69	48.2	31.2	10.7	0.9	–	9.0
Westmeath	72	42.3	33.6	11.4	–	–	12.7
Wexford	69	39.8	30.1	21.3	0.5	–	8.3
Wicklow	61	36.7	29.1	23.4	4.0	0.2	6.6
Total	68	41.6	34.9	11.5	1.2	0.2	10.6

COUNTY BOROUGH

County	Voter Turnout	Fianna Fáil	Fine Gael	Labour	Sinn Féin	Aontacht Éireann	Others
Cork	53	43.6	32.7	13.0	5.7	–	5.0
Dublin	40	30.8	26.9	20.0	2.1	–	20.2
Limerick	63	29.3	28.4	25.3	–	–	17.0
Waterford	66	30.2	23.0	15.5	10.3	1.4	19.6
Total	45	33.0	27.9	18.9	3.1	0.1	17.0

TABLE A.3 NUMBER OF SEATS WON, AND CANDIDATES, BY PARTY, 1979 LOCAL ELECTIONS

County	Total	Fianna Fáil	Fine Gael	Labour	Sinn Féin	Others
Carlow	21–43	8–19	9–14	3–7	0–0	1–3
Cavan	25–45	12–18	11–17	0–0	0–1	2–9
Clare	31–63	17–29	9–16	2–3	0–2	3–13
Cork	46–90	21–31	19–30	3–11	1–5	2–13
Donegal	28–63	11–19	10–18	0–0	1–3	6–23
Dublin	36–107	12–34	14–31	9–21	0–2	1–19
Galway	31–64	15–26	11–21	1–5	0–1	4–11
Kerry	26–47	14–16	7–17	2–5	0–1	3–8
Kildare	21–54	9–19	8–15	4–10	0–2	0–8
Kilkenny	26–64	11–23	10–23	4–12	1–4	0–2
Laoighis	25–46	11–20	12–19	2–3	0–0	0–4
Leitrim	22–35	10–14	10–14	0–0	0–0	2–7
Limerick	27–47	15–23	11–17	0–3	0–0	1–4
Longford	21–45	8–16	9–17	0–0	0–2	4–10
Louth	26–68	10–21	8–17	2–11	1–4	5–15
Mayo	31–57	15–23	16–23	0–2	0–1	0–8
Meath	29–64	13–23	9–19	5–14	0–1	2–7
Monaghan	20–35	9–12	8–13	0–0	0–3	3–7
Offaly	21–41	10–14	9–16	1–4	0–1	1–6
Roscommon	26–46	12–18	12–19	0–2	0–0	2–7
Sligo	24–47	10–15	11–20	1–2	0–1	2–9
Tipperary NR	21–41	9–18	8–12	3–7	0–0	1–4
Tipperary SR	26–54	11–19	8–18	4–9	0–1	3–7
Waterford	23–44	11–19	11–16	1–4	0–2	0–3
Westmeath	23–47	10–18	9–18	3–7	0–0	1–4
Wexford	21–53	10–15	7–16	2–11	0–2	2–9
Wicklow	21–50	7–18	8–16	4–11	1–2	1–3
Total	698–1460	311–540	274–492	56–164	5–41	52–223

COUNTY BOROUGH						
County	Total	Fianna Fáil	Fine Gael	Labour	Sinn Féin	Others
Cork	31–84	13–29	12–24	4–16	1–9	1–6
Dublin	45–174	12–42	15–38	11–31	1–11	6–52
Limerick	17–55	6–22	5–14	4–11	0–1	2–7
Waterford	15–39	5–9	4–9	2–5	2–6	2–10
Total	108–352	36–102	36–85	21–63	4–27	11–75
Total County & County Borough	806–1812	347–642	310–578	77–227	9–68	63–298

TABLE A.4 TURNOUT AND PARTY PREFERENCE BY COUNTY, 1979 LOCAL
ELECTIONS (%)

County	Voter Turnout	Fianna Fáil	Fine Gael	Labour	Sinn Féin	Others
Carlow	68	35.4	42.4	18.7	–	3.5
Cavan	75	42.4	41.9	–	0.2	15.5
Clare	71	50.7	28.3	4.5	0.5	16.0
Cork	72	39.4	38.4	10.7	4.2	7.3
Donegal	75	38.6	30.5	–	2.8	28.1
Dublin	51	30.3	37.9	22.2	0.8	8.8
Galway	64	46.8	32.0	6.3	1.2	13.7
Kerry	74	44.7	29.7	12.5	1.9	11.2
Kildare	61	41.3	31.2	17.6	1.6	8.3
Kilkenny	71	41.0	37.6	14.8	4.4	2.2
Laoighis	72	46.5	45.5	6.4	–	1.6
Leitrim	81	41.9	45.3	–	–	12.8
Limerick	72	56.3	36.3	3.3	–	4.1
Longford	79	41.7	38.9	–	1.4	18.0
Louth	65	33.7	29.6	10.8	3.1	22.8
Mayo	72	48.3	44.5	0.8	0.6	5.8
Meath	64	41.3	28.4	21.0	0.2	9.1
Monaghan	77	41.6	38.1	–	1.5	18.8
Offaly	67	42.3	43.1	6.0	0.3	8.3
Roscommon	77	47.6	42.0	1.0	–	9.4
Sligo	74	40.7	42.8	2.4	0.6	13.5
Tipperary NR	76	43.8	31.1	18.0	–	7.1
Tipperary SR	75	32.5	33.8	20.7	0.2	12.8
Waterford	69	43.3	47.7	4.4	2.8	1.8
Westmeath	69	45.8	34.2	13.2	–	6.8
Wexford	66	39.0	33.5	13.7	0.8	12.4
Wicklow	60	35.1	32.8	22.0	5.9	4.2
Total	67	41.1	36.2	10.5	1.5	10.7

COUNTY BOROUGH

County	Voter Turnout	Fianna Fáil	Fine Gael	Labour	Sinn Féin	Others
Cork	57	39.8	35.4	15.8	4.8	4.2
Dublin	48	27.1	29.3	18.3	4.9	20.4
Limerick	60	35.0	29.1	22.5	0.8	12.6
Waterford	68	26.6	23.9	11.2	20.0	18.3
Total	51	30.1	30.1	17.9	5.3	16.6

TABLE A.5 NUMBER OF SEATS WON, AND CANDIDATES, BY PARTY, 1985
LOCAL ELECTIONS

County	Total	Fianna Fáil	Fine Gael	Labour	Workers' Party	Othe
Carlow	21–42	10–19	7–13	3–5	0–1	1–
Cavan	25–40	14–18	10–16	0–0	0–0	1–
Clare	32–58	17–27	8–15	2–3	0–1	5–1
Cork	48–82	24–32	19–29	2–8	1–3	2–1
Donegal	29–62	11–19	9–17	0–2	1–1	8–2
Dublin Fingal	26–80	13–22	8–18	2–14	2–6	1–2
South Dublin	25–60	14–20	7–16	3–8	0–4	1–1
Dún Laoghaire	28–84	13–23	11–22	3–14	1–6	0–1
Galway	30–59	17–25	9–19	0–1	0–2	4–1
Kerry	27–51	13–18	7–12	3–6	0–3	4–1
Kildare	25–57	10–21	7–15	5–10	1–2	2–
Kilkenny	25–52	11–20	10–20	3–7	0–0	1–
Laoighis	25–52	14–22	9–19	1–5	0–0	1–
Leitrim	22–36	10–15	8–14	0–0	0–0	4–
Limerick	28–50	18–22	10–19	0–3	0–0	0–
Longford	21–38	10–15	9–15	0–0	0–0	2–
Louth	26–62	12–22	8–16	2–9	0–3	4–1
Mayo	31–55	15–25	14–23	0–2	0–0	2–
Meath	29–66	17–23	7–19	3–13	0–2	2–
Monaghan	20–34	10–13	7–11	0–0	0–1	3–
Offaly	21–45	12–16	6–15	0–6	0–0	3–
Roscommon	26–48	13–19	8–20	0–0	0–0	5–
Sligo	25–52	11–22	9–19	1–3	0–0	4–
Tipperary NR	21–38	12–16	6–12	1–8	0–0	2–
Tipperary SR	26–55	14–19	8–16	3–8	0–3	1–
Waterford	23–45	11–18	10–15	2–5	0–2	0–
Westmeath	23–58	13–19	5–19	3–9	0–0	2–1
Wexford	21–50	11–14	6–11	1–7	0–3	3–1
Wicklow	24–62	13–17	5–17	4–14	1–6	1–
Total	753–1575	382–581	247–492	47–170	8–51	69–28

COUNTY BOROUGH						
County	Total	Fianna Fáil	Fine Gael	Labour	Workers' Party	Others
Cork	31–82	13–26	8–20	5–12	2–5	3–19
Dublin	52–181	26–44	13–30	2–28	6–16	5–63
Galway	15–36	6–12	5–9	1–6	2–2	1–7
Limerick	17–45	5–14	6–13	1–7	0–2	5–9
Waterford	15–38	5–10	4–8	2–3	2–5	2–12
Total	130–663	55–106	36–80	11–56	12–30	16–110

Total County & County Borough   883–2238   437–687   283–572   58–226   20–81   85–391

Note: Others – Sinn Féin won 10 seats and Independents 75.

TABLE A.6 TURNOUT AND PARTY PREFERENCE BY COUNTY, 1985 LOCAL ELECTIONS (%)

County	Voter Turnout	Fianna Fáil	Fine Gael	Labour	Workers' Party	Others
Carlow	61	44.3	29.7	18.7	0.5	6.8
Cavan	71	53.5	36.4	–	–	10.1
Clare	69	53.5	23.4	5.2	0.4	17.5
Cork	63	47.0	38.4	2.0	3.7	6.2
Donegal	69	35.9	29.6	0.7	2.2	31.6
Dublin Fingal	47	42.1	25.3	12.0	7.1	13.5
South Dublin	50	45.3	27.7	11.3	4.0	11.7
Dún Laoghaire	45	38.1	34.1	12.1	4.6	11.1
Galway	67	54.5	28	0.2	0.9	16.4
Kerry	74	46.7	24	11.1	2.4	15.8
Kildare	56	42.9	23.2	21.3	2.6	10.0
Kilkenny	68	44.8	35.4	10.7	4.4	4.7
Laoighis	68	50.3	35.7	6.1	–	7.9
Leitrim	82	45.3	34.6	–	–	20.1
Limerick	67	57.6	37.4	1.7	–	3.3
Longford	77	46.2	38.2	–	–	15.6
Louth	61	43.4	27.9	8.6	1.0	19.1
Mayo	73	52.6	39	0.8	–	7.6
Meath	60	50.6	25.2	11.6	1.5	11.1
Monaghan	73	44.2	33.5	–	0.8	21.5
Offaly	68	49.7	32.7	4.1	–	13.5
Roscommon	76	43.6	37.4	–	–	19.0
Silgo	71	45.6	37.9	2.9	–	13.6
Tipperary NR	73	52.8	29.1	12.6	–	5.5
Tipperary SR	71	43.8	28.9	12.0	2.9	12.4
Waterford	65	48.7	38.1	7.7	1.1	4.4
Westmeath	65	48.1	27.9	12.8	–	11.2
Wexford	62	46.3	28.3	8.3	1.8	15.3
Wicklow	60	40.6	26.7	18.2	6.3	8.2
Total	63	46.7	31.3	7.3	2.1	12.6

APPENDIX 1: ELECTORAL PERFORMANCE AT LOCAL ELECTIONS

COUNTY BOROUGH

County	Voter Turnout	Fianna Fáil	Fine Gael	Labour	Workers' Party	Others
Cork	47	41.1	26.9	10.6	5.7	15.7
Dublin	43	41.8	20.0	9.0	9.4	19.8
Galway	44	41.2	29.0	10.8	9.0	10.0
Limerick	56	28.0	34.3	11.7	1.8	24.2
Waterford	57	30.2	23.0	9.3	10.3	27.2
Total	45	39.8	23.0	9.6	8.3	19.3
Total County & County Borough		45.5	29.8	7.6	3.0	14.1

Note: Others – Sinn Féin 3.3 per cent, Independents 10.8 per cent.

TABLE A.7 NUMBER OF SEATS WON, AND CANDIDATES, BY PARTY, 1991
LOCAL ELECTIONS

County	Total	Fianna Fáil	Fine Gael	Labour	Prog. Dems.	Workers' Party	Others
Carlow	21–43	9–18	7–13	4–6	1–1	0–0	0–5
Cavan	25–43	11–18	9–15	0–1	0–0	0–0	5–9
Clare	32–63	17–25	8–15	1–5	1–5	0–0	5–13
Cork	48–104	19–29	20–28	4–8	1–10	1–7	3–22
Donegal	29–62	11–19	9–15	1–1	0–0	1–1	7–26
Dublin Fingal	24–63	8–12	6–14	5–9	1–6	0–5	4–17
South Dublin	26–80	7–22	6–13	4–13	4–6	3–6	2–20
Dún Laoghaire	28–72	8–21	7–16	5–7	2–6	3–7	3–15
Galway	30–64	14–24	10–14	0–1	4–7	0–1	2–17
Kerry	27–47	13–17	7–12	4–7	0–1	0–0	3–10
Kildare	25–70	8–20	7–13	3–11	2–5	1–3	4–18
Kilkenny	26–51	12–21	10–15	4–7	0–3	0–2	0–3
Laoighis	25–47	13–18	9–17	1–5	1–2	0–0	1–5
Leitrim	22–37	9–14	9–12	0–0	0–0	0–0	4–11
Limerick	28–51	13–17	10–14	1–3	4–11	0–0	0–6
Longford	21–32	9–12	8–12	0–0	0–1	0–0	4–7
Louth	26–75	12–23	6–15	2–9	2–4	0–1	4–23
Mayo	31–56	15–22	13–19	1–4	0–3	0–0	2–8
Meath	29–62	12–22	9–13	4–11	0–3	1–2	3–11
Monaghan	20–33	8–12	7–9	0–0	0–0	0–1	5–11
Offaly	21–43	10–14	6–11	1–5	1–2	0–0	3–11
Roscommon	26–45	10–20	11–16	0–0	0–0	0–0	5–9
Sligo	25–51	11–21	11–14	0–3	0–1	0–0	3–12
Tipperary NR	21–40	11–15	7–11	2–6	0–5	0–0	1–3
Tipperary SR	26–52	10–19	9–13	4–9	0–4	0–1	3–6
Waterford	23–46	10–19	9–13	3–5	0–2	1–2	0–5
Westmeath	23–58	12–19	6–16	4–9	0–2	0–1	1–11
Wexford	21–40	8–14	8–10	1–7	0–2	0–1	4–6
Wicklow	24–62	9–16	4–9	5–10	0–5	1–6	5–16
Total	753–1528	319–552	248–407	64–16	224–97	12–47	86–336

COUNTY BOROUGH

County	Total	Fianna Fáil	Fine Gael	Labour	Prog. Dems.	Workers' Party	Others
Cork	31–82	9–19	6–17	6–8	3–6	3–7	4–25
Dublin	52–171	20–41	6–26	10–15	1–6	5–18	10–65
Galway	15–42	4–11	4–7	2–6	4–7	0–2	1–9
Limerick	17–46	2–12	4–9	5–8	3–6	1–2	2–9
Waterford	15–32	3–8	2–5	3–3	2–3	3–6	2–7
Total	130–373	38–91	22–64	26–40	13–28	12–35	19–115

Total County & County Borough

	883–1901	357–643	270–471	90–202	37–125	24–92	105–451

Note: Others – Green Party won 13 seats, Sinn Féin 7 and Independents 85.

TABLE A.8 TURNOUT AND PARTY PREFERENCE BY COUNTY, 1991 LOCAL
ELECTIONS (%)

County	Voter Turnout	Fianna Fáil	Fine Gael	Labour	Prog. Dems.	Workers' Party	Others
Carlow	58	39.3	31.0	23.3	2.5	–	3.9
Cavan	66	42.8	35.5	1.2	–	–	20.5
Clare	65	48.5	21.6	7.3	6.1	–	16.5
Cork	59	36.6	35.4	6.1	5.5	4.3	12.1
Donegal	61	36.2	24.7	2.3	–	2.5	34.3
Dublin Fingal	49	31.7	20.2	17.5	7.1	4.1	19.4
South Dublin	41	29.1	18.5	17.4	9.1	8.7	17.2
Dún Laoghaire	42	30.3	23.8	12.6	8.2	10.9	14.2
Galway	63	44.9	28.0	0.5	10.8	0.6	15.2
Kerry	66	44.1	26.2	16.6	0.7	–	12.4
Kildare	49	33.4	20.8	17.7	6.9	3.8	17.4
Kilkenny	64	43.2	33.3	16.0	3.0	2.0	2.5
Laoighis	65	49.3	34.1	7.2	4.1	–	5.3
Leitrim	76	43.4	35.4	–	–	–	21.2
Limerick	64	43.3	32.1	4.1	15.5	–	5.0
Longford	62	37.5	40.7	–	1.3	–	20.5
Louth	56	37.0	21.2	12.0	4.6	0.7	24.5
Mayo	68	47.3	39.9	3.6	2.8	-	6.4
Meath	51	44.8	26.5	11.8	3.1	2.9	10.9
Monaghan	65	40.1	32.8	–	–	1.0	26.1
Offaly	61	41.4	31.1	6.8	4.1	–	16.6
Roscommon	73	40.2	40.3	–	–	–	19.5
Sligo	68	44.4	34.3	3.3	1	–	17.0
Tipperary NR	68	45.4	35.9	10.1	3.8	–	4.8
Tipperary SR	66	37.9	27.2	18.8	4.4	1.2	10.5
Waterford	63	43.3	32.3	14.0	3.1	2.7	4.6
Westmeath	60	43.8	27.3	18.3	1.8	0.1	8.7
Wexford	58	40.2	30.2	12.6	2.5	2.1	12.4
Wicklow	57	32.2	14.6	19.2	3.4	5.3	25.3
Total	58	39.6	28.7	9.8	4.7	2.4	14.8

COUNTY BOROUGH

County	Voter Turnout	Fianna Fáil	Fine Gael	Labour	Prog. Dems.	Workers' Party	Others
Cork	52	29.0	18.8	14.2	8.4	9.9	19.7
Dublin	43	33.0	14.0	12.8	3.4	9.4	27.4
Galway	49	27.4	20.2	13.2	22.1	2.9	14.2
Limerick	57	20.3	22.0	22.9	13.1	3.6	18.1
Waterford	61	19.0	13.3	10.6	8.2	22.0	16.9
Total	46	29.9	15.9	14.5	6.7	9.4	23.6
Total County & County Borough	56	37.9	26.4	10.6	5.1	3.7	16.4

Note: Others – Green Party 2.4 per cent, Sinn Féin 2 per cent, Independents 12 per cent.

TABLE A.9 NUMBER OF SEATS WON, AND CANDIDATES, BY PARTY, 1999 LOCAL ELECTIONS

County	Total	Fianna Fáil	Fine Gael	Labour	Prog. Dems.	Workers' Party	Green Party	Sinn Féin	Others
Carlow	21–37	9–15	7–12	3–7	1–1	0–0	1–2	0–0	0–0
Cavan	25–48	13–17	9–15	0–1	0–0	0–0	0–1	2–4	1–10
Clare	32–65	18–26	9–17	0–6	1–1	0–0	0–2	0–1	4–12
Cork	48–101	19–29	21–30	4–11	1–3	0–0	0–6	0–4	3–18
Donegal	29–76	14–20	8–18	1–5	0–1	0–0	0–1	0–5	6–26
Dún Laoghaire	28–60	10–15	8–14	6–10	3–5	0–0	1–6	0–1	0–9
Fingal	24–58	6–16	5–10	6–9	1–2	0–0	1–6	0–1	5–14
Galway	30–57	16–22	9–16	0–1	2–3	0–0	0–0	0–1	3–14
Kerry	27–56	12–20	6–13	3–8	0–0	0–0	0–1	1–3	5–11
Kildare	25–62	9–17	5–12	5–12	2–2	0–0	0–4	0–1	4–14
Kilkenny	26–48	12–19	11–14	1–6	0–1	0–1	0–3	0–0	2–4
Laoighis	25–49	14–19	10–15	0–5	0–0	0–0	0–0	0–1	1–9
Leitrim	22–36	10–14	8–14	0–1	0–0	0–0	0–0	2–4	2–3
Limerick	28–55	14–22	10–13	0–2	3–6	0–0	0–3	0–1	1–8
Longford	21–35	8–16	10–11	0–1	1–1	0–0	0–0	0–0	2–6
Louth	26–62	14–19	7–15	1–8	0–2	0–1	0–4	1–5	3–8
Mayo	31–57	16–23	13–20	1–1	0–0	0–0	0–3	0–2	1–8
Meath	29–55	14–20	11–16	0–8	0–0	0–0	0–2	1–1	3–8
Monaghan	20–35	8–12	6–9	0–1	0–0	0–0	0–2	6–7	0–4
Offaly	21–34	9–14	7–11	1–3	0–0	0–0	0–0	0–1	4–15
Roscommon	26–49	9–19	12–16	0–1	1–2	0–0	0–1	0–0	4–10
Sligo	25–45	9–17	11–15	2–5	0–2	0–0	0–0	1–1	2–5
South Dublin	26–63	8–16	3–9	7–10	2–5	0–2	1–5	2–4	3–12
North Tipp	21–36	12–16	5–10	1–5	0–0	0–0	0–0	0–1	3–4
South Tipp	26–54	12–18	9–13	1–9	0–2	0–0	0–0	0–0	4–12
Waterford	23–48	11–19	8–12	3–7	0–1	0–1	0–1	0–1	1–6
Westmeath	23–39	12–16	6–11	5–7	0–0	0–0	0–0	0–0	0–5
Wexford	21–41	9–13	8–12	1–6	0–0	0–0	0–2	0–4	3–4
Wicklow	24–50	8–15	6–11	5–9	0–0	0–0	1–3	0–2	4–10
Total	753–1511	335–340	248–404	57–165	18–41	0–5	5–58	16–59	74–297

APPENDIX 1: ELECTORAL PERFORMANCE AT LOCAL ELECTIONS

CITY COUNCIL

County	Total	Fianna Fáil	Fine Gael	Labour	Prog. Dems.	Workers' Party	Green Party	Sinn Féin	Others
Cork	31–73	12–18	8–15	5–11	2–4	0–3	1–6	1–5	2–11
Dublin	52–133	20–36	9–20	14–19	0–5	0–6	2–13	4–7	3–27
Galway	15–42	5–9	4–7	2–6	4–6	0–0	0–2	0–1	0–11
Limerick	17–49	6–12	5–8	3–10	0–5	0–0	0–1	0–1	3–12
Waterford	15–32	4–6	3–6	2–4	1–1	3–6	0–3	0–0	2–6
Total	130–329	47–81	29–56	26–50	7–21	3–15	3–25	5–14	10–67
Total City & County Council	883–1840	382–421	277–460	83–205	25–62	3–18	8–83	21–73	84–364

Note: Others – Socialist Party 2 seats, Republican Sinn Féin 1 and Independents 81.

TABLE A.10 TURNOUT AND PARTY PREFERENCE BY COUNTY, 1999 LOCAL
ELECTIONS (%)

County	Fianna Fáil	Fine Gael	Labour	Prog. Dems.	Workers' Party	Green Party	Sinn Féin	Other
Carlow	36.4	31.3	18.6	4.5	0.0	3.7	0.0	5.
Cavan	45.8	37.4	0.7	0.0	0.0	0.5	8.5	6.
Clare	51.2	26.7	3.1	2.0	0.0	1.7	1.0	14.
Cork	38.6	38.3	10.2	2.6	0.0	1.1	1.9	7.
Donegal	41.5	22.8	3.7	1.0	0.0	0.2	4.4	25.
Fingal	27.2	20.8	19.2	4.2	0.0	8.3	1.4	19.
South Dublin	29.8	16.0	15.9	8.6	1.5	5.8	7.8	14.
Dún Laoghaire	31.6	27.3	18.1	7.9	0.0	7.3	1.2	6.
Galway	44.3	31.6	1.4	5.9	0.0	0.0	0.6	15.
Kerry	40.1	23.4	14.3	0.0	0.0	0.4	6.0	15.
Kildare	33.8	17.7	19.1	3.7	0.0	3.8	1.1	20.
Kilkenny	44.5	34.3	11.3	0.8	0.8	1.9	0.0	6.
Laois	50.2	33.0	4.2	0.0	0.0	0.0	1.7	10.
Leitrim	43.2	41.6	1.8	0.0	0.0	0.0	7.9	5.
Limerick	46.0	32.4	1.9	9.9	0.0	0.7	0.8	8.
Longford	42.7	41.3	0.3	4.1	0.0	0.0	0.0	11.
Louth	40.1	26.0	7.3	2.0	0.6	3.6	9.6	10.
Mayo	46.2	41.4	1.8	0.0	0.0	0.6	1.5	8.
Meath	45.1	30.4	6.7	0.0	0.0	1.6	2.1	14.
Monaghan	38.5	26.1	0.7	0.0	0.0	1.8	24.9	7.
Offaly	38.0	26.5	9.4	0.0	0.0	0.0	1.7	24.
Roscommon	36.8	38.9	0.9	2.7	0.0	0.2	0.0	20.
Sligo	35.2	39.1	9.4	0.7	0.0	0.0	4.0	11.
North Tipperary	46.9	26.1	9.0	0.0	0.0	0.0	1.4	16.
South Tipperary	40.2	28.1	12.3	1.8	1.3	0.0	0.0	16.
Waterford	43.5	30.0	15.6	1.6	0.0	1.5	0.2	7.
Westmeath	45.0	25.1	25.8	0.0	0.0	0.0	0.0	4.
Wexford	36.8	33.4	12.9	0.0	0.0	1.5	4.6	10.
Wicklow	33.1	21.5	20.6	0.0	0.0	3.7	2.0	19.
Total	39.9	29.6	9.8	2.5	0.1	1.9	3.1	13.

CITY COUNCIL

County	Fianna Fáil	Fine Gael	Labour	Prog. Dems.	Workers' Party	Green Party	Sinn Féin	Others
Cork	36.9	22.1	14.6	6.5	1.7	5.6	4.3	8.2
Dublin	34.7	17.8	17.7	2.5	1.9	7.7	7.9	9.8
Galway	29.6	18.0	12.2	21.5	0.0	3.0	1.1	13.9
Limerick	27.8	26.4	18.1	7.0	0.0	0.3	0.8	15.8
Waterford	20.2	20.5	13.6	3.8	16.7	3.4	0.0	10.9
Total	33.1	19.5	16.6	5.6	2.4	6.1	5.5	6.4
Total City & County Council	38.9	28.1	10.8	2.9	0.5	2.5	3.5	12.9

Note: Others – Socialist Party 0.4 per cent, Christian Solidarity Party 0.1 per cent, Socialist Workers' Party 0.1 per cent, Republican Sinn Féin 0. 1 per cent, Independents 12.3 per cent.

TABLE A.11 NUMBER OF SEATS WON, AND CANDIDATES, BY PARTY, 2004 LOCAL ELECTIONS

County	Total	Fianna Fáil	Fine Gael	Labour	Prog. Dems.	Green Party	Sinn Féin	Inds	Other
Carlow	21–45	8–15	7–13	4–7	1–1	1–5	0–1	0–3	0–0
Cavan	25–38	11–15	11–15	0–1	0–0	0–0	3–5	0–2	0–0
Clare	32–65	15–23	10–15	1–4	0–4	1–5	0–3	5–11	0–0
Cork	48–102	16–28	24–31	5–13	0–2	0–10	1–7	2–11	0–0
Donegal	29–67	14–22	8–15	0–2	0–1	0–4	4–6	3–17	0–0
Fingal	24–70	4–14	5–13	6–10	1–6	3–6	1–4	2–10	2–7
South Dublin	26–62	6–18	3–8	7–11	2–4	2–6	3–7	2–6	1–2
Dún Laoghaire	28–56	7–14	9–12	6–10	1–5	4–6	0–3	1–3	0–3
Galway	30–80	10–23	10–16	1–2	3–6	0–2	1–5	5–16	0–0
Kerry	27–61	11–18	8–14	2–8	0–1	0–2	2–6	3–12	0–0
Kildare	25–68	10–18	7–14	4–12	0–3	1–6	0–1	3–14	0–0
Kilkenny	26–50	8–17	11–17	5–7	0–1	1–3	0–2	1–3	0–0
Laois	25–52	11–18	9–14	1–3	1–8	0–1	1–2	2–6	0–0
Leitrim	22–34	10–13	8–12	0–1	0–0	0–1	2–4	2–3	0–0
Limerick	28–67	12–21	12–19	1–5	3–6	0–3	0–3	0–10	0–0
Longford	21–45	8–15	11–11	0–2	0–4	0–1	0–4	2–8	0–0
Louth	26–64	9–17	7–14	1–5	0–6	0–4	5–8	4–10	0–0
Mayo	31–61	12–22	15–23	1–2	0–1	0–1	1–2	2–10	0–0
Meath	29–63	12–19	9–15	0–6	0–1	1–6	2–6	5–10	0–0
Monaghan	20–34	5–11	7–10	0–0	0–0	0–0	7–8	1–5	0–0
Offaly	21–50	8–13	6–14	0–3	2–6	0–2	0–2	5–10	0–0
Roscommon	26–56	9–18	10–17	0–2	0–2	0–3	1–3	6–11	0–0
Sligo	25–45	10–17	10–15	3–5	0–0	0–0	1–4	1–4	0–0
North Tipp	21–42	10–14	5–9	2–7	0–0	0–0	0–2	4–10	0–0
South Tipp	26–59	10–18	8–14	2–7	0–3	0–1	0–4	6–12	0–0
Waterford	23–52	7–17	11–14	4–8	0–1	0–1	1–2	0–9	0–0
Westmeath	23–47	9–16	8–11	6–11	0–0	0–2	0–5	0–2	0–0
Wexford	21–55	6–14	7–17	1–7	0–1	0–2	3–4	4–9	0–1
Wicklow	24–61	6–14	7–14	6–8	0–4	1–4	0–5	4–12	0–0
Total	753–1644	274–505	263–426	69–169	14–77	15–87	39–118	76–249	3–13

APPENDIX 1: ELECTORAL PERFORMANCE AT LOCAL ELECTIONS

CITY COUNCIL

ounty	Total	Fianna Fáil	Fine Gael	Labour	Prog. Dems.	Green Party	Sinn Féin	Inds	Other
ork	31–61	11–15	8–12	6–7	1–3	1–6	2–6	1–9	1–3
ablin	52–139	12–31	10–21	15–21	1–8	1–13	10–16	3–16	0–13
alway	15–38	2–8	3–7	4–6	3–6	1–3	1–3	1–5	0–0
merick	17–47	2–9	5–7	4–5	0–7	0–1	0–2	6–14	0–2
aterford	15–32	1–6	4–6	3–3	0–2	0–2	2–3	3–6	2–4
•tal	130–317	28–69	30–53	32–42	5–26	3–25	15–30	14–50	3–22

•tal City
County 883–1961 302–574 293–479 101–211 19–103 18–112 54–148 90–299 6–37
•uncil

ote: Others – Socialist Party 4 seats, Workers' Party 2.

TABLE A.12 TURNOUT AND PARTY PREFERENCE BY COUNTY, 2004 LOCAL ELECTIONS (%)

County	Turn-out	Fianna Fáil	Fine Gael	Labour	Prog. Dems.	Green Party	Sinn Féin	Inds	Oth
Carlow	55	36.3	32.9	17.2	3.4	6.9	1.5	1.8	–
Cavan	66	41.2	44.0	0.8	–	–	11.6	2.5	–
Clare	63	41.5	28.8	3.3	3.8	4.5	1.9	16.1	–
Cork	63	32.9	37.2	10.2	1.3	4.3	6.1	8.0	–
Donegal	60	40.0	23.0	1.1	0.6	2.2	13.5	19.6	–
Fingal	55	21.5	22.5	18.7	6.0	8.2	5.2	8.2	9.7
South Dublin	52	25.7	13.7	18.5	6.7	8.4	13.5	9.7	3.9
Dún Laoghaire	54	24.9	24.1	20.3	8.4	10.3	3.7	4.5	3.9
Galway	62	34.5	28.1	3.4	9.0	0.7	4.0	20.2	–
Kerry	66	37.5	24.8	11.5	0.6	1.0	7.9	16.7	–
Kildare	51	32.0	20.8	18.9	3.8	6.1	0.7	17.7	–
Kilkenny	62	34.0	38.2	14.8	1.8	4.6	2.7	4.0	–
Laois	64	37.8	33.9	4.1	10.1	0.7	3.8	9.7	–
Leitrim	73	40.1	38.1	2.2	–	0.6	11.2	7.8	–
Limerick	62	38.6	38.1	3.8	8.2	2.0	1.5	7.8	–
Longford	70	35.3	38.9	1.8	6.9	0.5	3.7	12.9	–
Louth	57	29.7	23.4	4.7	3.9	4.7	16.9	16.8	–
Mayo	64	37.0	43.2	2.3	1.4	0.5	4.2	11.5	–
Meath	53	38.4	26.6	6.5	1.1	4.3	9.5	13.6	–
Monaghan	68	29.4	29.9	–	–	–	31.1	9.7	–
Offaly	62	33.8	29.3	3.9	7.2	0.8	1.3	23.8	–
Roscommon	69	36.2	35.9	1.9	2.5	0.7	2.9	20.1	–
Sligo	68	37.4	36.8	10.4	–	–	7.7	7.7	–
North Tipperary	67	41.3	21.5	10.3	–	–	2.9	24.0	–
South Tipperary	65	34.9	27.9	9.6	1.4	1.2	4.1	21.0	–
Waterford	62	35.9	36.2	14.6	1.0	1.8	3.0	7.5	–
Westmeath	59	35.3	31.1	25.1	–	1.1	5.1	2.3	–
Wexford	58	30.4	33.1	8.8	1.1	2.0	8.9	15.4	0.1
Wicklow	60	25.0	22.5	21.8	3.5	4.7	6.7	15.9	–
Total	60	33.5	29.3	10.2	3.5	3.6	6.7	12.4	1.0

CITY COUNCIL

County	Turn-out	Fianna Fáil	Fine Gael	Labour	Prog. Dems.	Green Party	Sinn Féin	Inds	Oth.
Cork	55	29.1	22.1	13.2	4.7	6.8	10.4	9.2	4.5
Dublin	52	23.2	16.9	20.5	3.6	6.4	18.5	7.9	3.0
Galway	53	19.2	17.1	16.5	22.6	7.3	8.4	7.0	–
Limerick	56	15.9	26.6	14.0	8.4	0.3	3.8	30.0	1.0
Waterford	59	13.9	18.5	15.2	3.0	4.2	13.6	21.2	10.5
Total	53	22.8	18.6	18.1	5.7	6.0	14.9	10.6	3.3
Total City & County Council	50	31.8	27.7	11.4	3.8	3.9	8.0	12.1	1.3

Note: Others – Socialist Party 0.8 per cent, Socialist Workers' Party 0.3 per cent, Workers' Party 0.2 per cent, Christian Solidarity Party 0.01 per cent.

APPENDIX 2

Local Election Data

To discover the motives of local election candidates, a mail survey was conducted by one of the authors immediately after the 2004 local elections. In addition, candidates were asked to return a sample of their election literature. The survey was a 4-page questionnaire with 35 questions sent by post to 556 of the 1,665 party candidates and to each of the 297 Independent candidates. Independents received a slightly different version that had an extra five questions pertaining specifically to their Independent status. The reason for the particular emphasis on Independents was due to it being the focus of a previous study by Weeks. Because there is sometimes a difference in behaviour between urban and rural candidates, 353 surveys were sent to party candidates for county councils, and 203 for those running in city councils. Ensuring the inclusion of a reasonable number of both city and county candidates was necessary for the controlling of particular effects that might be unique to a particular locale.

The quantity to survey from each party was based on its number of candidates as a proportion of total candidacies in city and county councils. This was done to ensure a reasonable weighting of responses so that one party would be not overly represented in the final data set. The party respondents were chosen at random from a list of their party's candidates within the two separate forms of councils. Details of the numbers of questionnaires sent and returned according to party affiliation are detailed below in table A.1.

TABLE A.13 DISTRIBUTION AND SURVEY RESPONSE RATE FROM LOCAL ELECTION CANDIDATES

Party	Surveyed	Respondents	% Response Rate
Fianna Fáil	183	95	51.9
Fine Gael	150	94	62.7
Labour	72	48	66.7
Prog. Dems.	43	26	62.8
Green Party	49	24	49.0
Sinn Féin	40	24	60.0
Independent	297	179	60.3
Others	19	14	73.7
Total	853	504	59.1

Source: 2004 local election candidate survey.

The questionnaire was posted one week after the elections, and was followed up by a reminder postcard three weeks later to those who had not yet returned it. Two weeks after this, the questionnaire was re-sent to all respondents yet to reply. This labour-intensive procedure produced a very satisfactory final response rate of 59 per cent. The response rate is of particular importance when making inferences from surveys. A low response rate means that there is an increased probability of the sample data being not randomly selected; that is, those who did respond may not be reflective of the random sample originally drawn. Consequently, the random sampling error can increase, resulting in unreliable findings. Such biases are less likely to occur in a candidate survey because of the low levels of heterogeneity amongst same party candidates (as opposed to voters), reducing the variance in the sample. In any case, the reasonable response rates means that unreliable findings are less likely to occur, especially considering the rates being larger to other candidate surveys. This hypothesis was checked – replicating the methodology of a previous study[1] – by comparing party vote share and turnout in the constituencies with respondents to the national mean. We do not have the room to detail these findings here, but the figures were quite similar, indicating that the campaigns covered by the sample survey are very representative of all campaigns. Finally, the questionnaire is detailed over the next four pages.

UNIVERSITY OF DUBLIN
DEPARTMENT OF POLITICAL SCIENCE
TRINITY COLLEGE
DUBLIN 2, IRELAND

Code
Number

LOCAL ELECTION CANDIDATE SURVEY 2004

I am conducting research in the Department of Political Science on local election candidates and their campaigns. I would be very grateful if you could complete this questionnaire and return it, as soon as possible, in the pre-paid envelope to the Department of Political Science at Trinity College, Dublin. ALL ANSWERS WILL BE TREATED AS STRICTLY CONFIDENTIAL. The identity of our respondents will never be revealed to any outside body and the information you give me will be used only for research purposes. THANK YOU FOR YOUR HELP.

Most questions will require you to put a tick (✓) in a single box or series of boxes. For example:

Strongly agree........ ☐₁   Agree ....☐₂   Disagree............ ☐₃   Strongly disagree .... ☐₄

Q1. Thinking back to the time you decided to run as a local election candidate, why did you choose to run for election? How important were the following reasons in motivating your decision to run for election? Can you please rank how important each of these reasons were on a scale of 1-10 where 1 means 'not at all important' and 10 means 'extremely important' [Please tick (✓) one box on each line]

	Not at all Important								→ Extremely Important	
Asked to run by party	☐₁	☐₂	☐₃	☐₄	☐₅	☐₆	☐₇	☐₈	☐₉	☐₁₀
Asked to run by a group/organisation	☐₁	☐₂	☐₃	☐₄	☐₅	☐₆	☐₇	☐₈	☐₉	☐₁₀
To highlight an important issue	☐₁	☐₂	☐₃	☐₄	☐₅	☐₆	☐₇	☐₈	☐₉	☐₁₀
To win a seat	☐₁	☐₂	☐₃	☐₄	☐₅	☐₆	☐₇	☐₈	☐₉	☐₁₀
Interested in politics	☐₁	☐₂	☐₃	☐₄	☐₅	☐₆	☐₇	☐₈	☐₉	☐₁₀
To represent local area	☐₁	☐₂	☐₃	☐₄	☐₅	☐₆	☐₇	☐₈	☐₉	☐₁₀
To continue family representation in political life	☐₁	☐₂	☐₃	☐₄	☐₅	☐₆	☐₇	☐₈	☐₉	☐₁₀
For the excitement of a political race	☐₁	☐₂	☐₃	☐₄	☐₅	☐₆	☐₇	☐₈	☐₉	☐₁₀
To achieve certain values important for society	☐₁	☐₂	☐₃	☐₄	☐₅	☐₆	☐₇	☐₈	☐₉	☐₁₀
Other reasons *(please write below)*	☐₁	☐₂	☐₃	☐₄	☐₅	☐₆	☐₇	☐₈	☐₉	☐₁₀

Q2. What were the most important issues that you highlighted in your campaign? *(Please write below)*
Issue 1_____
Issue 2_____
Issue 3_____

Q3. Thinking back to when you decided to run for election, how long before polling day on June 11 did you make this decision? *(Please write here)* _____

Q4. Turning towards your active campaign to win a seat, how long did this last? [Please tick (✓) one box only]

Less than one month ....☐₁
1 month ....☐₂
2 months.....................................☐₃
3 months.....................................☐₄
4 months ....☐₅
5 months ....☐₆
6 months ....☐₇
More than 6 months.....................................☐₈

Q5. How far advanced would you say your campaign preparation was when the election was officially called on May 13th? Please indicate on a scale of 0-10 where 0 means 'no preparation' and 10 means 'all preparation' for your campaign was completed? *(Please circle the score corresponding to your view)*

No Preparation | | | | | | | | | | Preparation completed
| 0 | 1 | 2 | 3 | 4 | 5 | 6 | 7 | 8 | 9 | 10 |

Q6. What was the average number of volunteer workers you had on a typical campaign day? *(Please write below)*
_____

Q7. Approximately how many people in total would you say helped in your campaign? *(Please write below)*
_____

Q8. Thinking back to the beginning of your campaign, what percentage of the local election constituency (Local Electoral Area) did your campaign team plan to cover? [Please tick (✓) one box only]
0%☐ 10%☐ 20%☐ 30%☐ 40%☐ 50%☐ 60%☐ 70%☐ 80%☐ 90%☐ 100%☐

Q9. Did you target your campaign to appeal to specific categories of voters, e.g. women, young people, farmers, etc.?
No ☐₁ ⟶GO TO Q10
Yes ☐₂ ....If Yes, please describe the categories of voters below
_____

Q10. Thinking back to the types of people who supported you in the election, which types of people do you think voted for you at the election? [Please tick (✓) all that apply]
People living near your home .... ☐₁
People you'd met personally .... ☐₂
People who were concerned with a particular issue which you campaigned on .... ☐₃
People supporting the party you were standing for .... ☐₄
People from a particular social group (please specify group(s) below) .... ☐₅

Other groups of people (please write below) .... ☐₆

Q11. Once your election campaign got underway, approximately how much of your time was devoted to the campaign?
[Please tick (✓) one box only]
0%☐　10%☐　20%☐　30%☐　40%☐　50%☐　60%☐　70%☐　80%☐　90%☐　100%☐

Q12. In approximately what percentage of households in your Local Electoral Area did you personally make face-to-face contact with one or more occupant(s)? [Please tick (✓) one box only]
0%☐　10%☐　20%☐　30%☐　40%☐　50%☐　60%☐　70%☐　80%☐　90%☐　100%☐

Q13. In approximately what percentage of households in your Local Electoral Area did your campaign team make face-to-face contact with one or more occupant(s)? [Please tick (✓) one box only]
0%☐　10%☐　20%☐　30%☐　40%☐　50%☐　60%☐　70%☐　80%☐　90%☐　100%☐

Q14. What types of election activities did you undertake to promote your campaign? [Please tick (✓) all boxes that apply]
Door-to-door canvassing .... ☐₁　　Spoke on radio.. ☐₆
Distributed election material on the street ...... ☐₂　　Television appearances.................................. ☐₇
Sent letters or postcards to voters .... ☐₃　　Press conferences... ☐₈
Telephone canvassing .... ☐₄　　Spoke at public meeting(s)............................ ☐₉
Put up posters .... ☐₅　　Organised public rallies................................. ☐₁₀

Q15. How many election leaflets did you distribute during your campaign?_____

Q16. How many election posters did you put up during your campaign?_____

Q17. Approximately what proportion of the local electorate did you distribute leaflets to? [Please tick (✓) one box only]
0%☐　10%☐　20%☐　30%☐　40%☐　50%☐　60%☐　70%☐　80%☐　90%☐　100%☐

Q18. Approximately what proportion of the time spent on your electoral campaign was devoted to each of the following activities? [Please tick (✓) one box for each activity]

Campaign Activity	0%	10%	20%	30%	40%	50%	60%	70%	80%	90%	100%
Door-to-door canvassing	☐₁	☐₁	☐₂	☐₃	☐₄	☐₅	☐₆	☐₇	☐₈	☐₉	☐₁₀
Distributing leaflets, putting up posters	☐₁	☐₁	☐₂	☐₃	☐₄	☐₅	☐₆	☐₇	☐₈	☐₉	☐₁₀
Walking the streets to meet & greet people	☐₁	☐₁	☐₂	☐₃	☐₄	☐₅	☐₆	☐₇	☐₈	☐₉	☐₁₀
Dealing with the media	☐₁	☐₁	☐₂	☐₃	☐₄	☐₅	☐₆	☐₇	☐₈	☐₉	☐₁₀
Attending public & political meetings	☐₁	☐₁	☐₂	☐₃	☐₄	☐₅	☐₆	☐₇	☐₈	☐₉	☐₁₀
Attending publicity and PR events	☐₁	☐₁	☐₂	☐₃	☐₄	☐₅	☐₆	☐₇	☐₈	☐₉	☐₁₀

Q19. How important a role did computers play in your election campaign? [Please tick (✓) one box for each answer]
Did your campaign organisation have a designated computer specialist/expert? .... Yes☐₁　No☐₂
Did you use a computerised electoral register?... Yes☐₁　No☐₂
Did you use a computer to monitor voters canvassed and responses received? .... Yes☐₁　No☐₂
Did you use a computer for correspondence with voters, e.g. to print letters and address labels?...... Yes☐₁　No☐₂
Did you promote your campaign on the Internet? .... Yes☐₁　No☐₂

Q20. Did you use an electoral register in the organisation of your campaign? [Please tick (✓) one box only]
Yes .... ☐₁　　No........☐₂ →Go to Q22

Q20a. What did you use the electoral register for? [Please tick (✓) all boxes that apply]
To send personal letter to voters... ☐₁
Maintain records of voters canvassed and responses received .... ☐₂
Draw up list of potential supporters amongst electorate.................................. ☐₃
Other uses (Please state below).. ☐₅

APPENDIX 2: LOCAL ELECTION DATA

Q21. Thinking back to polling day, did you or your campaign team perform any of the following activities?
[Please tick (✓) all boxes that apply]   **Q23a. How many helped out with this activity?**

Bringing voters to the polling station	☐₁ →go to Q23a	_____
Distributing last-minute leaflets	☐₂ →go to Q23a	_____
Door-to-door canvassing	☐₃ →go to Q23a	_____
Telephone canvassing	☐₄ →go to Q23a	_____
Driving around Local Electoral Area in loudspeaker van	☐₅ →go to Q23a	_____
Monitor turnout of potential supporters at polling stations	☐₆ →go to Q23a	_____

Q22. Thinking of your profile in your Local Electoral Area, how well-known would you consider yourself on a scale of 1-10, where '1' means 'not at all known' and '10' means 'extremely well-known'? [Please tick (✓) one box only]

	Not at all known ──────────────────────────────── Extremely well-known
How well known are you locally?	☐₁ ☐₂ ☐₃ ☐₄ ☐₅ ☐₆ ☐₇ ☐₈ ☐₉ ☐₁₀

Q23. How important are the following factors in influencing the extent of your local profile? Please rank the importance of each of the following factors on a scale of 1-10, where 1 means 'not at all important' and 10 means 'extremely important'. [Please tick (✓) one box for each factor]

	Not at all Important ──────────────────→ Extremely Important
Your job	☐₁ ☐₂ ☐₃ ☐₄ ☐₅ ☐₆ ☐₇ ☐₈ ☐₉ ☐₁₀
A career in politics	☐₁ ☐₂ ☐₃ ☐₄ ☐₅ ☐₆ ☐₇ ☐₈ ☐₉ ☐₁₀
Sporting prowess	☐₁ ☐₂ ☐₃ ☐₄ ☐₅ ☐₆ ☐₇ ☐₈ ☐₉ ☐₁₀
History of involvement in local campaigns	☐₁ ☐₂ ☐₃ ☐₄ ☐₅ ☐₆ ☐₇ ☐₈ ☐₉ ☐₁₀
Other reasons *(Please state below)*	☐₁ ☐₂ ☐₃ ☐₄ ☐₅ ☐₆ ☐₇ ☐₈ ☐₉ ☐₁₀

Q24. How important are the following factors in explaining the vote you attracted at the 2004 local elections: your personality, your policies, your party label, your record of constituency work, your election campaign, or your family having a record of involvement in politics? Please rank the importance of each of the following factors on a scale of 1-10, where 1 means 'not at all important' and 10 means 'extremely important'. [Please tick (✓) one box for each factor]

	Not at all Important ──────────────────→ Extremely Important
Personality	☐₁ ☐₂ ☐₃ ☐₄ ☐₅ ☐₆ ☐₇ ☐₈ ☐₉ ☐₁₀
Policies	☐₁ ☐₂ ☐₃ ☐₄ ☐₅ ☐₆ ☐₇ ☐₈ ☐₉ ☐₁₀
Party label	☐₁ ☐₂ ☐₃ ☐₄ ☐₅ ☐₆ ☐₇ ☐₈ ☐₉ ☐₁₀
Record of constituency work	☐₁ ☐₂ ☐₃ ☐₄ ☐₅ ☐₆ ☐₇ ☐₈ ☐₉ ☐₁₀
Election campaign	☐₁ ☐₂ ☐₃ ☐₄ ☐₅ ☐₆ ☐₇ ☐₈ ☐₉ ☐₁₀
Record of family involvement in politics	☐₁ ☐₂ ☐₃ ☐₄ ☐₅ ☐₆ ☐₇ ☐₈ ☐₉ ☐₁₀
Other reasons *(please state below)*	☐₁ ☐₂ ☐₃ ☐₄ ☐₅ ☐₆ ☐₇ ☐₈ ☐₉ ☐₁₀

Q25. Aside from your 2004 local election campaign, have you ever been involved in any <u>other</u> political campaign(s)? Please refer to both election and issue campaign(s). [Please tick (✓) one box only]

No.................. ☐₁ →GO TO Q28
Yes.................. ☐₂ If Yes, please describe the type of campaign(s) below

_____

Q26. Which one of the following statements most accurately reflected your confidence in winning a seat at the local elections? [Please tick (✓) one box only]

I felt fairly certain of winning	☐₁
I thought I could win, but I felt the election would be close	☐₂
I thought the election could go either way	☐₃
I expected to lose, but I thought if I worked, I could make it a close race	☐₄
I felt fairly certain of losing	☐₅

Q27. People often talk about a left-wing vs. a right-wing dimension in politics. On a scale of 1-10 where 1 stands for extreme left-wing and 10 for extreme right-wing, where would you place yourself on this scale?
(Please circle the score corresponding to your view)

Extreme Left									Extreme Right
1	2	3	4	5	6	7	8	9	10

Q28. Please indicate how strongly you agree or disagree with each of the following two statements.
The best rule in voting is to pick the best candidate, regardless of party label. [Please tick (✓) one box only]
Strongly agree........ ☐₁   Agree .... ☐₂   Disagree............ ☐₃   Strongly disagree .... ☐₄

Q29. It doesn't really matter which political party is in power, in the end things go on much the same [Please tick (✓) one box only]
Strongly agree........ ☐₁   Agree .... ☐₂   Disagree............ ☐₃   Strongly disagree .... ☐₄

QUESTIONS FOR INDEPENDENT CANDIDATES (QI-QV)

QI. At the 2004 local election, did you seek a nomination to be a candidate for any political party? [Please tick (✓) one box only]

Yes .. ☐₁   No........ ☐₂ → go to QII

QIa. If Yes, which party did you seek a nomination from? [Please tick (✓) one box only]

Fianna Fáil ☐₁	Progressive Democrats ☐₅
Fine Gael ☐₂	Sinn Féin ☐₆
Green Party ☐₃	Other party (please specify below) ☐₇
Labour ☐₄	

QII. Have you ever been a member of a political party? [Please tick (✓) one box only]

Yes .... ☐₁   No........ ☐₂ → go to QIV

QIIa. Which party were you a member of? [Please tick (✓) one box only]

Fianna Fáil ☐₁	Progressive Democrats ☐₅
Fine Gael ☐₂	Sinn Féin ☐₆
Green Party ☐₃	Other party (please specify below) ☐₇
Labour ☐₄	

QIII. When did you leave the party? Please write year in boxes ☐☐☐☐

QIV. For how many years were you a member of the party? *(Please write below)*

QV. There are many different types of Independents. Which of the following best describes you? [Please tick (✓) one box only]

Independent Republican ☐₁	Single-issue Independent ☐₆
Independent Party Rebel ☐₂	Right-wing Independent ☐₇
Independent standing for an interest group ☐₃	Constituency Independent ☐₈
Independent Farmer ☐₄	Other type of Independent (please describe) ☐₉
Left-wing Independent ☐₅	

Q30. Thinking about your experience of campaigns, apart from your 2004 local election campaign:
Q30a. Have you ever sought a nomination to contest elections to positions in any of the following bodies? [Please tick (✓) all that apply]
Q30b. Have you ever stood for office in any of the following bodies? [Please tick (✓) all that apply]
Q30c. Have you ever held a post in any of the following bodies? [Please tick (✓) all that apply]

	(Q30a) Sought nomination	(Q30b) Stood for office	(Q30c) Held post
Town/County/City Council	☐₁	☐₂	☐₃
Dáil	☐₁	☐₂	☐₃
Post within party	☐₁	☐₂	☐₃

Q31. At the time of the 2004 local election were you a member of any of the following groups?
[Please tick (✓) all that apply]   **Q31a.** Did any of these groups support your campaign?

Local community/residents' association	☐₁ → go to Q31a	Yes ☐₁ ... No ☐₂
Irish Farmers' Association or other farming association	☐₁ → go to Q31a	Yes ☐₁ ... No ☐₂
The GAA	☐₁ → go to Q31a	Yes ☐₁ ... No ☐₂
A trade union (please specify)	☐₁ → go to Q31a	Yes ☐₁ ... No ☐₂
Professional organisation (please specify)	☐₁ → go to Q31a	Yes ☐₁ ... No ☐₂

Q32. Do you live in a rural area or village, in a small or middle size town, or in a large town or city? [Please tick (✓) one box only]

Rural area or village .... ☐₁   Small or middle size town ..... ☐₂   Large town or city .... ☐₃

Q33. Which of the following best describes the highest level of education you have achieved to date? [Please tick (✓) one box only]

None ... ☐₁   Completed Primary ... ☐₂   Junior/Inter Cert/equivalent... ☐₃   Leaving Cert/equivalent... ☐₄
Diploma/Certificate ... ☐₅   University Degree/equivalent... ☐₆   Masters/equivalent ... ☐₇   PhD/equivalent ... ☐₈

Q34. What is/was your occupation, outside of politics? If appropriate, please state the rank or grade, for example, Civil Service, Gardaí, etc. If proprietor or manager, please state the number of people employed. If farmer please state acreage farmed.

Q35. In what year were you born? Please write year in boxes ☐☐☐☐

THANK YOU FOR TAKING THE TIME TO COMPLETE THIS SURVEY
PLEASE RETURN IT IN THE FREEPOST ENVELOPE SUPPLIED
NO STAMP IS NECESSARY

References

Chapter 1 – The Importance of Local Government and Local Elections

1. A similar point is made regarding British local elections by Colin Rallings and Michael Thrasher (1997), *Local Elections in Britain*, London: Routledge.

2. David Wilson and Chris Game (2002), *Local Government in the United Kingdom* (3rd edition), Houndmills, Basingstoke: Palgrave Macmillan, p. 38.

3. L.J. Sharpe (1970), 'Theories and Values of Local Government', *Political Studies*, 18: 2, pp. 153–174, p. 160.

4. Kevin B. Smith, Alan Greenblatt and John Buntin (2005), *Governing States and Localities*, Washington DC: CQ Press.

5. Mark Callanan (2003), 'The Role of Local Government' in Mark Callanan and Justin F. Keogan (eds.), *Local Government in Ireland: Inside Out*, Dublin: Institute of Public Administration, pp. 3–13.

6. George Jones and John Stewart (1985), *The Case for Local Government*, London: Allen & Unwin, p. 5.

7. Wilson and Game, as per 2 above, p. 5.

Chapter 2 – The Irish Local Government System

1. Bríd Quinn (2003), 'Irish Local Government in a Comparative Context' in Mark Callanan and Justin F. Keogan (eds.), *Local Government in Ireland: Inside Out*, Dublin: Institute of Public Administration, p. 453.

2. Indecon International Economic Consultants (2005), *Review of Local Government Financing*, report commissioned by the Minister for the

Environment, Heritage and Local Government, Dublin: Government Publications, p. i.

3. OECD (2008), *Ireland – Towards an Integrated Public Service*, Paris: OECD.

4. Mary Daly (2001), 'The County in Irish History' in Mary Daly (ed.), *County & Town – One Hundred Years of Local Government in Ireland*, Dublin: Institute of Public Administration, p. 3.

5. Virginia Crossman (1994), *Local Government in Nineteenth-Century Ireland*, Belfast: Institute of Irish Studies, Queen's University Belfast, p. 6.

6. Desmond Roche (1982), *Local Government in Ireland*, Dublin: Institute of Public Administration, pp. 32–33.

7. Virginia Crossman, as per 5 above, p. 4.

8. *Ibid*. p. 5.

9. *Ibid*. p. 97.

10. Desmond Roche, as per 6 above, p. 46.

11. Tom Barrington (1991), 'Local Government in Ireland' in Richard Batley and Gerry Stoker (eds.), *Local Government in Europe*, Basingstoke: Macmillan, p. 157.

12. See Bill Kissane (2002), *Explaining Irish Democracy*, Dublin: University College Dublin Press.

13. Desmond Roche, as per 6 above, p. 53.

14. Aodh Quinlivan (2006), *Philip Monahan, A Man Apart: The Life and Times of Ireland's First Local Authority Manager*, Dublin: Institute of Public Administration, p. 68.

15. Tom Barrington, as per 11 above, p. 157.

16. Mary Daly (1997), *The Buffer State: The Historical Roots of the Department of the Environment*, Dublin: Institute of Public Administration, p. 297.

17. Tom Barrington, as per 11 above, p. 158.

18. Gerard Dollard (2003), 'Local Government Finance: The Policy Context' in Mark Callanan and Justin F. Keogan (eds.), *Local Government in Ireland: Inside Out*, Dublin: Institute of Public Administration, p. 331.

19. KPMG (1996), *The Financing of Local Government in Ireland*, report commissioned by the Department of the Environment, Dublin: Government Publications.

20. Aodh Quinlivan (2000), 'Local Government Bill, 2000 – Implications for Municipal Authorities. Another False Pregnancy?', *Administration*, 48(3), pp. 10–20.

21. OECD Report, as per 3 above, p. 68.

22. Muiris MacCárthaigh and Mark Callanan (2008), 'Transforming Public Services – A Strengthened Role for Local Government', *Local Authority Times*, vol. 12 (4), p. 9.

23. Aodh Quinlivan (2008), 'Reconsidering Directly Elected Mayors in Ireland: Experiences from the United Kingdom and America, *Local Government Studies*, 34 (5), p. 619.

Chapter 3 – Local Elections: The Rules of the Game

1. F. S. L. Lyons (1971), *Ireland Since the Famine*, Princeton: Scribner Publishing.

2. Richard Haslam (2003), 'The Origins of Irish Local Government' in Mark Callanan and Justin F. Keogan (eds.), *Local Government in Ireland: Inside Out*, Dublin: Institute of Public Administration, p. 27.

3. Diarmaid Ferriter (2001), *Lovers of Liberty – Local Government in 20th Century Ireland*, Dublin: National Archives of Ireland, p. 37.

4. *Eagle and Cork County Advertiser*, 29 April 1899.

5. Ferriter, as per 3 above, p. 36.

6. John Coakley (2001), 'Local Elections and National Politics' in Mary Daly (ed.), *County & Town – One Hundred Years of Local Government in Ireland*, Dublin: Institute of Public Administration, p. 81.

7. *Ibid*. p. 80.

8. Peter Greene (2003), 'Local Elections' in Mark Callanan and Justin F. Keogan (eds.), *Local Government in Ireland: Inside Out*, Dublin: Institute of Public Administration, p. 99.

9. See article by Vincent Browne in *The Village*, 20 March 2007.

Chapter 4 – Local Elections, 1899–2004

1. Both of these pre-election stories come from Diarmaid Ferriter (2001), *Lovers of Liberty – Local Government in 20th Century Ireland*, Dublin: National Archives of Ireland, p. 36.

2. *Ibid.* p. 2.
3. This information comes from a local elections exhibition put together by the Local Authority Archivists' Group.
4. *Ibid.*
5. *Ibid.*
6. John Coakley (2001), 'Local Elections and National Politics' in Mary Daly (ed.), *County & Town – One Hundred Years of Local Government in Ireland*, Dublin: Institute of Public Administration, p. 78.
7. Aodh Quinlivan (2006), *Philip Monahan, A Man Apart: The Life and Times of Ireland's First Local Authority Manager*, Dublin: Institute of Public Administration, p. 27.
8. John Coakley, as per 6 above.
9. *Ibid.*
10. As quoted in *The Irish Times* of 15 June 1979.
11. As quoted in *The Irish Times* of 1 July 1991.
12. *The Irish Times* of 14 June 1999.
13. Liam Kenny (1999), *From Ballot Box to Council Chamber*, Dublin: Institute of Public Administration, p. 21.
14. Liam Kenny (2004), *From Ballot Box to Council Chamber*, Dublin: Institute of Public Administration, p. 6.
15. Adrian Kavanagh (2004), 'The 2004 Local Elections in the Republic of Ireland', *Irish Political Studies*, 19 (2), p. 83.

Chapter 5 – Local Election Candidates

1. Pippa Norris and Joni Lovenduski (1995), *Political Recruitment, Gender, Race and Class in the British Parliament,* Cambridge: Cambridge University Press.
2. Dermot Keogh (2008), *Jack Lynch: A Biography*, Dublin: Gill & Macmillan, p. 1.
3. Thomas A. Kazee (ed.) (1994), *Who runs for Congress? Ambition, Context, and Candidate Emergence.* Washington: Congressional Quarterly Inc., p 165.
4. Shirley Williams and Edward L. Lascher Jr. (eds.) (1993), *Ambition and Beyond: Career Paths of American Politicians.* Berkeley, CA: Institute of Governmental Studies Press, p. 71.

5. Carl O'Brien (2004), 'Two candidates have the same name, but one doesn't want any votes.' *The Irish Times*, 1 June.

6. Basil Chubb (1963), 'Going about persecuting civil servants.' *Political Studies* 10(3): 272–86.

7. F. W. Ridley, and Grant Jordan (eds.) (1999), *Protest Politics: Cause Groups and Campaigns.* Oxford: Oxford University Press.

8. Mary Kerrigan (2004), *That's Politics! A guide to politics in Ireland*, Dublin: Mary Kerrigan, p. 28.

9. Source: *Bowman on Sunday*, RTÉ Radio 1, 18 January 2009.

10. Chris Game and David Wilson (2002), *Local Government in the United Kingdom* (3rd ed.), Basingstoke: Palgrave, p. 256.

11. Howard Elcock (1994), *Local government: policy and management in local authorities* (3rd ed.), London: Routledge.

12. R. Baxter (1972), 'The Working Class and Labour Politics', *Political Studies* 20, p. 106, cited in Elcock, as per 11 above, p. 73.

13. Maud Committee Report (1967), *The Management of Local Government*, London: HMSO, p. 163 cited in Elcock, p. 71.

14. Michael Marsh, Richard Sinnott, John Garry and Fiachra Kennedy (2008), *The Irish Voter*, Manchester: Manchester University Press.

15. Marsh et al, as per 14 above, p. 202.

16. Amir Abedi (ed.) (2004), *Anti-Political Establishment Parties: A Comparative Analysis*, London: Routledge, pp. 92–5.

17. J. F. Zimmerman (1976), 'Role Perceptions of Irish City and County Councillors', *Administration*, vol. 24 (4); Siobhan Carey (1986), 'Role perceptions among county councillors', *Administration* 34 (3), pp. 302–16.

Chapter 6 – Local Election Campaigns

1. Pippa Norris (2002), 'Do campaign communications matter for civic engagement? American elections from Eisenhower to George W. Bush' in David M. Farrell and Rüdiger Schmitt-Beck (eds.), *Do Political Campaigns Matter? Campaign effects in elections and referendums*, London: Routledge, p. 128.

2. David M. Farrell and Rüdiger Schmitt-Beck (2002), 'Studying political campaigns and their effects' in Farrell and Schmitt-Beck, as per 1 above, p. 9.

3. Norris, as per 1 above.

4. Paul F. Lazarsfeld and Bernard Berelson, and Hazel Gaudet (1968), *The people's choice: how the voter makes up his mind in a presidential campaign* (3rd ed.), New York: Columbia University Press.

5. Peter Mair (1987), *The Changing Irish Party System: Organisation, Ideology and Electoral Competition,* London: Frances Pinter, pp. 110–111.

6. David M. Farrell (1994), 'Ireland: centralisation, professionalisation and competitive pressures' in Richard S. Katz and Peter Mair, *How Parties Organise,* London: Sage, p. 221.

7. David Denver and Gordon Hands (1997), *Modern Constituency Electioneering: Local Campaigning in the 1992 General Election,* London: Frank Cass, p. 248.

8. Rachel K. Gibson, Michael Margolis, David Resnick and Stephen Ward (2003), 'Election campaigning on the WWW in the US and the UK: A comparative analysis' *Party Politics* 9 (1), p. 50.

9. Stephen Gundle (1992) 'Italy' in David Butler and Austin Ranney (eds.), *Electioneering: A Comparative Study of Continuity and Change,* Oxford: Clarendon, pp. 194–5.

10. Seán Fleming, Paul Bradford, Joan Burton, Fiona O'Malley, Dan Boyle, Aengus Ó Snódaigh, and Liam Twomey (2003), 'The candidates' perspective' in Michael Gallagher, Michael Marsh, and Paul Mitchell (eds.), *How Ireland Voted 2002,* London: Palgrave Macmillan, p. 60.

11. David M. Farrell (2004), 'Before campaigns were "modern": Irish electioneering in times past' in Tom Garvin, Maurice Manning, and Richard Sinnott (eds.), *Dissecting Irish Politics: Essays in Honour of Brian Farrell,* Dublin: University College Dublin Press, pp. 178–98.

12. Maol Muire Tynan, 'Pedalling the Green machine through a disenchanted world', *The Irish Times,* 18 June 1991.

13. Marie O'Halloran, 'Gormley to announce halving of poll-spend limit to €15,000', *The Irish Times,* 8 February 2009.

14. Ken Benoit and Michael Marsh (2003a), 'For a Few Euros more: Campaign Spending Effects in the Irish Local Elections of 1999' in *Party Politics* 9(5), pp. 561–82; Ken Benoit and Michael Marsh (2003b) 'Campaign spending in the local government elections of 1999' in *Irish Political Studies* 18(2), pp. 1–22.

15. Denver and Hands, as per 7 above, pp. 248–9.

Chapter 7 – Local Electoral Behaviour, 1967–2004

1. Charlie McCreevy, ' "Roscommon factor" spells trouble for the major parties', *The Irish Times*, 1 July 1991.
2. McCreevy, as per 1 above.
3. Diarmaid Ferriter (2004), *The transformation of Ireland*, *1900–2000*, London: Profile, p. 366.
4. McCreevy, as per 1 above.
5. Michael Gallagher (1989), 'Local Elections and Electoral Behaviour in the Republic of Ireland', *Irish Political Studies* 4, p. 26.
6. R. K. Carty (1981), *Party and parish pump. Electoral politics in Ireland*, Ontario: Wilfrid Laurier, pp. 106–107.
7. Denis Coghlan, 'FG aims to poll "as close as possible" to 1979 result, *The Irish Times*, 5 June 1985.
8. Ella Shanahan and Willy Clingan, 'FF TDs told to stand in local elections', *The Irish Times*, 15 April 1985.
9. Noel Whelan, 'Doyle's retirement shatters FG hopes of two European seats', *The Irish Times*, 10 January 2009.
10. Gallagher, as per 2 above.
11. Gallagher, as per 2 above, p. 31.
12. Seán Donnelly (1999), *Elections 99 – All kinds of everything*, Dublin: Seán Donnelly, p. 62
13. Liam Weeks (2007), 'Candidate selection: democratic centralism or managed democracy' in Michael Gallagher and Michael Marsh (eds.), *How Ireland Voted 2007*, London: Palgrave, p. 60.
14. Michael Gallagher (1990), 'The election results and the new Dáil' in Michael Gallagher and Richard Sinnott (eds.), *How Ireland Voted 1989*, Galway: Centre for the Study of Irish Elections in association with PSAI Press, p. 87; Michael Gallagher (1993), 'The election of the 27th Dáil' in Michael Gallagher and Michael Laver (eds.), *How Ireland Voted 1992*, Dublin: PSAI Press, p. 73; Mary-Clare O'Sullivan (1999), 'The social and political characteristics of the twenty-eighth Dáil' in Michael Marsh and Paul Mitchell (eds.), *How Ireland Voted 1997*, Boulder, Colorado: Westview Press, p. 191; Michael Gallagher (2003), 'Stability and turmoil: analysis of the results' in Michael Gallagher, Michael Marsh, and Paul Mitchell (eds.), *How Ireland Voted 2002*, London: Palgrave, p. 114.
15. *The Irish Times*, 18 September 1923.

Epilogue

1. *The Irish Times,* 15 April 1994.
2. Liam Weeks (2009), 'The parties and the party system' in John Coakley and Michael Gallagher (eds.), *Politics in the Republic of Ireland* (5th ed.), London: Routledge.

Appendix 1

1. In this and all other tables in this appendix, the data comes from official election results published by the Department of Environment and Local Government and Donnelly (1992, 1999).

Appendix 2

1. David Denver and Gordon Hands (1997), *Modern Constituency Electioneering: Local Campaigning in the 1992 General Election*, London: Frank Cass, pp. 322–323.

Bibliography

Barrington, Tom (1991), 'Local Government in Ireland' in Richard Batley and Gerry Stoker (eds.), *Local Government in Europe*, Basingstoke: Macmillan.

Baxter, R. (1972), 'The Working Class and Labour Politics', *Political Studies* 20.

Benoit, Ken, and Michael Marsh (2003a), 'For a Few Euros more: Campaign Spending Effects in the Irish Local Elections of 1999', *Party Politics* 9(5).

Benoit, Ken, and Michael Marsh (2003b) 'Campaign spending in the local government elections of 1999' *Irish Political Studies* 18(2).

Brennan, Louis (2000), *Count, Recount and Petition*, Dublin: Institute of Public Administration.

Callanan, Mark and Justin F. Keogan (eds.) (2003), *Local Government in Ireland: Inside Out*, Dublin: Institute of Public Administration.

Carey, Siobhan (1986), 'Role perceptions among county councillors', *Administration* 34(3), pp. 302–16.

Chubb, Basil (1963), 'Going about persecuting civil servants.' *Political Studies* 10(3): 272–86.

Collins, Neil (1987), *Local Government Managers at Work*, Dublin: Institute of Public Administration.

Crossman, Virginia (1994), *Local Government in Nineteenth-Century Ireland*, Belfast: Institute of Irish Studies, Queen's University Belfast.

Daly, Mary (1997), *The Buffer State: The Historical Roots of the Department of the Environment*, Dublin: Institute of Public Administration.

Daly, Mary (ed.) (2001), *County & Town – One Hundred Years of Local Government in Ireland*, Dublin: Institute of Public Administration.

Denver, David and Gordon Hands (1997), *Modern Constituency Electioneering: Local Campaigning in the 1992 General Election*, London: Frank Cass.

Department of the Environment (1974), *Local Elections, 1974*, Dublin: The Stationery Office.

Department of the Environment (1979), *Local Elections, 1979*, Dublin: The Stationery Office.

Department of the Environment (1985), *Local Elections, 1985*, Dublin: The Stationery Office.

Department of the Environment (1991), *Local Elections, 1991*, Dublin: The Stationery Office.

Department of the Environment (1996), *Better Local Government – A Programme for Change*, Dublin: The Stationery Office.

Department of the Environment and Local Government (1999), *Local Elections, 1999*, Dublin: The Stationery Office.

Department of the Environment and Local Government (2004), *Local Elections, 2004*, Dublin: The Stationery Office.

Donnelly, Seán (1992), *Poll position. An analysis of the 1991 local elections*, Dublin: Seán Donnelly.

Donnelly, Seán (1999), *Elections 99 – All kinds of everything*, Dublin: Seán Donnelly.

Elcock, Howard (1994), *Local government: policy and management in local authorities* (3rd ed.), London: Routledge.

Farrell, David M. (1994), 'Ireland: centralisation, professionalisation and competitive pressures' in Richard S. Katz and Peter Mair, *How Parties Organise*, London: Sage.

Farrell, David M. (2004), 'Before campaigns were "modern": Irish electioneering in times past' in Tom Garvin, Maurice Manning, and Richard Sinnott (eds.), *Dissecting Irish Politics: Essays in Honour of Brian Farrell*, Dublin: University College Dublin Press.

Farrell, David M. and Rüdiger Schmitt-Beck (2002), *Do political campaigns matter?* London: Routledge.

Ferriter, Diarmaid (2001), *Lovers of Liberty – Local Government in 20th Century Ireland*, Dublin: National Archives of Ireland.

Gallagher, Michael (1989), 'Local Elections and Electoral Behaviour in the Republic of Ireland', *Irish Political Studies* 4.

Game, Chris and David Wilson (2002), *Local Government in the United Kingdom* (3rd ed.), Basingstoke: Palgrave.

Hughes, Ian, Paula Clancy, Clodagh Harris and David Beetham (2007), *Power to the People: Assessing Democracy in Ireland*, Dublin: New Island.

Indecon International Economic Consultants (2005), *Review of Local Government Financing,* report commissioned by the Minister for the Environment, Heritage and Local Government, Dublin: Government Publications.

Jones, George and John Stewart (1985), *The Case for Local Government*, London: Allen & Unwin.

Kavanagh, Adrian (2004), 'The 2004 Local Elections in the Republic of Ireland', *Irish Political Studies*, 19(2).

Kazee, Thomas A. (ed.) (1994), *Who runs for Congress? Ambition, Context, and Candidate Emergence.* Washington: Congressional Quarterly Inc.

Kenny, Liam (1999), *From Ballot Box to Council Chamber*, Dublin: Institute of Public Administration.

Kenny, Liam (2004), *From Ballot Box to Council Chamber*, Dublin: Institute of Public Administration.

Kerrigan, Mary (2004), *That's Politics! A guide to politics in Ireland,* Dublin: Mary Kerrigan.

KPMG (1996), *The Financing of Local Government in Ireland*, report commissioned by the Department of the Environment, Dublin: Government Publications.

Lazarsfeld, Paul F., Bernard Berelson, and Hazel Gaudet (1968), *The people's choice: how the voter makes up his mind in a presidential campaign* (3rd ed.), New York: Columbia University Press.

Lyons, F.S.L. (1971), *Ireland Since the Famine*, Princeton: Scribner Publishing.

MacCárthaigh, Muiris and Mark Callanan (2008), 'Transforming Public Services – A Strengthened Role for Local Government', *Local Authority Times*, vol. 12(4).

Mair, Peter (1987), *The Changing Irish Party System: Organisation, Ideology and Electoral Competition,* London: Frances Pinter.

Marsh, Michael, Richard Sinnott, John Garry and Fiachra Kennedy (2008), *The Irish Voter,* Manchester: Manchester University Press.

Maud Committee Report (1967), *The Management of Local Government*, London: HMSO.

Nealon, Ted, Various, *Nealon's Guide to the Dáil and Seanad*; Dublin: Gill & Macmillan.

Norris, Pippa, and Joni Lovenduski (1995), *Political Recruitment, Gender, Race and Class in the British Parliament,* Cambridge: Cambridge University Press.

OECD (2008), *Ireland – Towards an Integrated Public Service*, Paris: OECD.

Quinlivan, Aodh (2000), 'Local Government Bill, 2000 – Implications for Municipal Authorities. Another False Pregnancy?' *Administration,* 48(3).

Quinlivan, Aodh (2006), *Philip Monahan, A Man Apart: The Life and Times of Ireland's First Local Authority Manager*, Dublin: Institute of Public Administration.

Quinlivan, Aodh (2008), 'Reconsidering Directly Elected Mayors in Ireland: Experiences from the United Kingdom and America', *Local Government Studies*, 34(5).

Quinlivan, Aodh and Neil Collins (2009), 'Multi-Level Governance' in John Coakley and Michael Gallagher (eds.), *Politics in the Republic of Ireland* (5th ed.), London: Routledge.

Quinlivan, Aodh and Emmanuelle Schön-Quinlivan, (2009), *Innovation and Best Practice in Irish Local Government*, Dublin: Chambers Ireland and SIPTU.

Rallings, Colin and Michael Thrasher (1997), *Local Elections in Britain*, London: Routledge.

Ridley, F. W., and Grant Jordan (eds.) (1999), *Protest Politics: Cause Groups and Campaigns.* Oxford: Oxford University Press.

Roche, Desmond (1982), *Local Government in Ireland*, Dublin: Institute of Public Administration.

Sharpe, L. J. (1970), 'Theories and Values of Local Government', *Political Studies*, 18(2).

Smith, Kevin B., Alan Greenblatt and John Buntin (2005), *Governing States and Localities*, Washington DC: CQ Press.

Weeks, Liam (2007), 'Candidate selection: democratic centralism or managed democracy' in Michael Gallagher and Michael Marsh (eds.), *How Ireland Voted 2007*, London: Palgrave.

Weeks, Liam (2009), 'We don't like (to) party. A typology of Independents in Irish political life', *Irish Political Studies* 24(1).

Weeks, Liam (2009), 'Political parties and the party system' in John Coakley and Michael Gallagher (eds.), *Politics in the Republic of Ireland* (5th ed.), London: Routledge.

Williams, Shirley and Edward L. Lascher Jr. (eds.) (1993), *Ambition and Beyond: Career Paths of American Politicians*. Berkeley, CA: Institute of Governmental Studies Press.

Wilson, David and Chris Game (2002), *Local Government in the United Kingdom* (3rd edition), Houndmills, Basingstoke: Palgrave Macmillan.

Zimmerman, J. F. (1976), 'Role Perceptions of Irish City and County Councillors', *Administration*, vol. 24 (4).

Zimmerman, J. F. (2006), 'Executive-Council Relations in England and Ireland', *Current Municipal Problems*, Vol.33, No.2.

Index